Medium Rare

Reminisce  'ant

Muriel Renard

Medium Rare
Reminiscences of a Clairvoyant

©1998 Muriel Renard

ISBN 186163 027 1

ALL RIGHTS RESERVED

Cover design by Paul Mason
Cover picture by Rohan Renard

Published by:

Capall Bann Publishing
Freshfields
Chieveley
Berks
RG20 8TF

Contents

... Unbeknown to me malevolent presences were silently invading my bedroom...

In the middle of the night I tossed around in bed... What was that loud thumping noise? Was it the sound of my heartbeats?

My subconscious mind was urging:

- "Come on, Muriel, hurry! W A K E   U P!"

Startled I sat up bolt straight in bed and stared around in the darkness. Something was moving... I didn't like the sound of it at all...

Cold and shivering I reached out for my bed jacket and wrapped it around my shoulders....

In the darkness I sat up alone facing the forces of Evil, gasping for air, choking... my heart beating violently at an increasing pace. Was I having a heart attack?

Something else was building up in the night... and it was taking what little power I had left in order to do so.

Clutching my chest, I thought I was going to pass out or die altogether.

The thumping noise was growing louder... I recognised it now - it was the sound of soldiers marching towards me... their boots treading rhythmically as they advanced...

What lay ahead? Transfixed, I waited...

1

Muriel Renard.
Photograph taken by Mukind Pandit

Introduction

W H A T... You are a medium?" People either stare in amazement or take a step back. Sometimes they giggle uncontrollably to cover their embarrassment, asking such inspired questions as: "Then tell me which horse is going to win the next race". Others pretend they haven't heard and immediately start talking nineteen to the dozen.

Some of my neighbours call me "The Witch" - they don't know the difference between a medium and a witch. In the old films mediums were invariably frauds who dressed in widows' weeds, laid their hands on the table before going into deep breathing and sighing sessions, calling out in agony: "Are you there, Auntie Flo?"... (No, dear. You've frightened the life out of her...she's run a mile).

- *"How did you know you had THESE POWERS?"* is a frequent question making me feel like the Witch in Snow White and the seven Dwarfs. It simply started off as a fascinating hobby after meeting other mediums and asking: "How do you do clairvoyance? Show me how it works." So I went for classes year after year and much to my delight it DID work! I learned to develop this gift and control it. Clairvoyance has also given me inner strength and changed my values.

- *"It's easy for you, you were born a medium".*

If this were true toddlers would give demonstrations of clairvoyance. As a child I could feel the presence of spirit people around me. At times they made me feel uneasy as I did not know how to cope with them. It was fear of the unknown but today ghosts don't worry me.

- *"Isn't it dangerous to dabble with the Occult?"*

Of course, it is although mediumship is not generally classified as "occult". But it is no more risky than driving a car on the motorway. If you can't drive then you have problems but when properly trained you become confident.

Clairvoyance is a gift of love: its purpose is to prove survival after death and to help others. It requires total dedication and the ability to set your own problems aside and listen.

Perhaps I should clarify just a few of the words I use in the book: a SENSITIVE is a person receptive to matters not visible to the naked eye; a CLAIRVOYANT

3

sees them while a CLAIRAUDIENT hears telepathic messages . A MEDIUM is specially trained to communicate with spirits. Some clairvoyants may perhaps only be able to read Tarot cards, using their intuition without necessarily being aware of the presence of spirits. So all mediums are clairvoyant while all clairvoyants may not necessarily be mediums too.

Another word is SPIRITS. Those mentioned in the book are people who have left their physical body at death and live on in another dimension. 'Spirit' as a collective word refers to the inhabitants of the Next World as a whole including angels, spirit guides etc. A SPIRIT GUIDE is a person who once lived on earth, is usually unrelated to the sitter but comes to guide them on a spiritual pathway. On the other hand they may also have been connected in a previous incarnation on earth. Guides are often nuns, monks, lamas, Native Americans, Chinese philosophers etc. - people who lived a simple, spiritual life. (I have never heard of a cowboy spirit guide!) They come to preach love rather than established religious dogmas.

A sister-of-mercy would normally inspire someone either to help others or to do spiritual drawings or writing. A Native American usually helps healers with their work. In a later chapter I mention that a friend of mine has a Zulu spirit guide. Why not an Indian? Probably because the Zulu felt an affinity with my friend's personality. Zamba (that is the guide's name) told me that he helps other people too.

A GHOST haunts a place and is stuck between this world and the next. This may be an old lady who lived in her house all her life and still carries on with her daily chores, unaware that she has passed on. The new owners terrify her. She thinks that THEY are the ghosts haunting her home. So it's the medium's task to contact her gently and show her the way to the Next World. Some ghosts are only pictures in time, empty shells as, for example, the proverbial Lady in Grey who walks up the castle turret at midnight

A POLTERGEIST is an energy dormant in a house which only manifests when one of the occupants is a restless child reaching puberty or anyone else with a tense, nervous disposition.

All these facts will be explained in more detail as we go along.

- *" It is wrong to call up the spirit of the dead"*

There are no dead. The body is discarded like an old overcoat and the person is free and well in another dimension where he or she is met by relatives and

4

friends. A spirit may wish to keep in touch with loved ones on earth and from time to time pops back to see how they are progressing and tries to help them. I certainly can't call up the spirits of any Tom, Dick or Harry unless they are already hovering around eagerly waiting to pass on a message.

- *"The Bible says it is evil"*

What nonsense! The Bible has been mistranslated with bits added and removed down the centuries. In Mark 9 Jesus himself contacted spirits. He secretly led three of his disciples, Peter, James and John up a lonely mountain where he became transfigured in a great white light. Elijah and Moses - who had died many generations before - appeared and talked to him. The whole interview would have been perfectly relaxed. However, the disciples were petrified as the average person would be today. When the meeting was over Jesus told them not to tell anyone as people were even more narrow-minded in those days than they are now.

- *"Can you see ghosts... spectres?... I think I'd die of fear"*

is another encouraging remark. Yes I do see them from time to time! Films on the Supernatural are usually scary. The producers make them spine chilling in order to draw the crowds and make money. In real life it's a different story altogether. I don't stand in the kitchen peeling potatoes while having a conversation with a spirit at the same time. Clairvoyance is something you switch on. When I "pull the plug out" I can't see anything.

Like attracts like. You will not attract evil spirits when you are not on their wavelength. Supposing you have a granddaughter you are very attached to. Suddenly you die. From the Next World you see her crying over a broken romance. You will come back and hover around her with words of comfort: *"Come on, don't be so upset. Someone much more caring will come along soon. I am still here with you and I care."* If your granddaughter starts screaming with fear when she perceives you you will feel totally dejected. Your ancestors do not hover around you all the time. They have to get on with their own life and only come back for special reasons. If you loved your grandmother when she was alive why should you be afraid of her when she has passed? She is the same person who still cares for you. Should you see her, just say: *"Hello, Gran. It's lovely to meet you. Pity I can't offer you a cup of tea"*. A reply should come telepathically in your mind. Don't expect profound words of wisdom from a being on a cloud, playing the harp. Your grandmother will make the same type of comments as she did on earth, she will look exactly the same but without wrinkles (hurray!) and remarkably fit and healthy.

5

Another comment is: *"I have had a dabble myself with an Ouija board"*.

Not a good idea. The average medium does not use this gadget. When handled correctly it does produce results but as a party trick to entertain guests it provides unprotected communication with the Next World. Departed relatives can come through the board, but so could the local junkie who died of an overdose, a sex maniac or, in fact, any unbalanced character who is stuck halfway between this world and the next and wishes to continue living on this earth by possessing a person who is still alive.

The glass or the table can go flying across the room , smashing against the wall.

Chapter One

Most of my neighbours are friendly but a few of them imagine I spend my time concocting potions in a cauldron and casting evil spells. They say "Hello" in the street and smile politely while looking me up and down suspiciously. (No, dear. You're quite safe, don't worry. I won't turn you into a bat).

Some born-again Christians would happily have me burnt at the stake for my own good. (Now, didn't Jesus preach something about loving Thy neighbour?).

My friend Jeannie became a Baptist and had every room in her flat exorcised... against my evil influence! No, it's not a joke - and now that her home is purified and protected by a poster in the hall advertising "Jesus loves you", she won't let me in anymore in case I 'pollute the atmosphere'. Trying to reason with her was a waste of time: "Look, I don't harm anyone but spend my time helping people, talking them out of committing suicide and trying to mend broken relationships". (Why did I bother?) But she was adamant: 'What you do is EVIL! Turn to Jesus and we'll be friends again'.

- *"But I am not against Jesus! I spend hours giving healing to people".*

- *'Oh, you work with the Devil in disguise who makes their health improve for a while in order to dupe them. However, rest assured that all your patients will eventually die a violent death'.* (Quite a collection by now I would imagine!)

Such brainwashing left me speechless. At first it was very upsetting being rejected by a good friend, all because of fanaticism. But now I just shrug my shoulders for it's her loss after all, not mine. Repeatedly I have met people who judge and condemn something without any knowledge of the subject. One Sunday I was sitting in a packed bus next to Susan, a pretty unmarried Mum, obviously another convert, because out of the blue she turned to me and said - loud enough for even the bus driver to hear:

- *'Muriel, you are a very kind person but you do the Devil's work'!* (Now how can I be both kind and evil at the same time?).

Immediately, we had the undivided attention of the other passengers, as all conversations stopped and ears were straining to catch a little of the dialogue. It would while away the time until they reached their destination.

Susan carried on, talking even louder, moved by her passion:

- *"What you do is EVIL and WICKED! Let me come and read out of the Bible to you".*

Out of the corner of my eye, I could see broad smiles as people nudged each other, delighted at the forthcoming entertainment. But alas, this was not to be. Sorry, but I spoilt their fun.

- *"My life is fine as it is, thank you, please let's change the subject".*

One elderly lady with a carrier bag on her lap leaned back, sighing: 'Aah..' in disappointment.

A few years later, believe it or not, there we were sitting next to each other on the bus again. This time, Susan had just had a row with her son and now she was sobbing on my shoulder, tears rolling down my new cream jacket as she told me the whole story:

- *"Muriel, I do everything for him! Why is he so ungrateful? You understand how hurt I feel having two sons yourself".* (The boy, apparently, refused to study and had stormed out of the house slamming the door behind him.) I tried to comfort her:

- *"Don't worry, your son is at a difficult age. He will grow up and one day you will be proud of him - you'll see".*

My companion had temporarily forgotten my malevolent activities as she sat there blowing her nose. By the time she got off the bus, Susan was smiling as, from the pavement she waved her wet handkerchief in farewell: maybe it was not the end of the world after all and there was hope left...

On another occasion, an elderly lady who would normally frown suspiciously and ignore me approached with a big smile on her face: *"Hello, Muriel dear, how are you?"* (Well, what do you know, life is full of surprises... she even knew my name!) Her blue eyes scrutinized me behind her National Health glasses: *"I hear you are a faith healer"*...

Pausing, she patted her head (there was not a hair out of place). *"My neighbour is dying of leukemia. The doctors say it's a matter of days. Could you pop over and heal her? Only don't tell her what you do do as she might not approve, her being a Roman Catholic, like".*

- '*So sorry to hear your friend is ill*', I answered, '*but at this stage it's too late - besides I cannot impose help on someone who would reject it.*'

The poor woman walked away quite disappointed.

Healing is usually a slow process which works very well especially with the patient's cooperation. It does not replace the doctor's treatment, but complements it. People tend to approach a healer as a last resort, when there is not much left to lose one way or another, and expect instant miracles. They think I simply have to put my hand on the sick person's head and, hey presto! cancer, Multiple Sclerosis, Parkinson's Disease etc. will vanish at once. Jesus managed to raise Lazarus from the dead so I refer those patients to him.

With regards to clairvoyance a medium is usually practical and down-to-earth - the only way to help others with their problems. It took me a few years to become wise and not let people walk all over me: now I don't! My feet remain firmly on the ground while I listen to the most hair raising tales, some of which turn out to be true, while others remain the colourful product of a fertile imagination.

At college I studied Accountancy, Languages and Business Studies - what a contrast! - but it was not a waste of time: I keep accounts efficiently, give readings in several languages and file papers away instead of stuffing them in a drawer. A steady, boring career in an office lay ahead and I soon realised that one can't give affection to a typewriter. For at retirement age, what would I have achieved?... 4O,000 letters typed over a period of years... just another faded memory filed away in the archives of time. Certainly, secretaries are invaluable to their companies, but it was not for me.

Life is eternal: nothing perishes. The spirits of various friends have stood at the foot of my bed waving good-bye as they were about to leave this world. It is always a wonderful experience seeing them look so well and happy, their illnesses and wrinkles gone. Death itself is nothing to fear. On various occasions I have held the hand of a dying person who looked up into space, smiling: "*Mum, how nice to see you*"... or: " *Oh, Fred, darling... I've missed you so much...*"

The first mediums I met amazed me. How could they possibly describe my ancestors: their appearance, occupation, mannerisms and even give me their names? Why could they see them when I could not? The details were incredibly accurate - there is no way they could have made them up.

For example, my Great-Aunt Louise was seen wearing a shawl and eating an apple. (She loved them). A large tabby cat lay asleep on her lap. A pot of Azaleas (her favourite flowers) stood on the table next to her. That was her to a "T"!

On another occasion a medium said: *'I have here a German soldier who does not see very well with one eye. His uniform is too large. I am getting the name 'Albert'. He is talking about Louise, his sweetheart - does that make any sense to you, Muriel?'*.

No, it did not!

- "*Well,*" the clairvoyant continued, "*Louise was a great aunt of yours*".

- "*Yes, that's correct*".

- "*As a young woman she went to Austria on holidays and fell in love with this man. Shortly afterwards, World War I was declared and Albert was called up in the army. She was forbidden to keep in touch with him. He died in active service. I am told Louise never married.*"

- "*I see, how interesting, the story is starting to make sense*".

- "*They are now happily reunited in the Spirit World*".

No one could have found that kind of information in a book. And as Auntie died years ago in Belgium that medium could not possibly have known her.

I asked several relatives to confirm this story but no one seemed to know. Finally another aunt stared at me in amazement: "*Well, this truly is astonishing. Louise did indeed have a German suitor called Albert. But when the war broke out he was called up and their courtship had to end. The young woman was never allowed to contact Albert again*".

Poor Auntie! I can just imagine the heartache she must have felt at the time. It was so nice to know she had found happiness at last. Fascinated, I was determined to find out more: "How do you do clairvoyance? Show me how it works". With enthusiasm I embarked on a course. It took me 12 years of training and perseverance to become a medium. Then I too could see! But the ensuing events exceeded my wildest expectations. I have attempted to write down some of these incredible experiences, all of which are true. So if you believe me, well and good. If you are sceptical it's quite understandable. All I know is that I am telling the truth and that's all that matters.

There are anecdotes concerning some of my unusual or eccentric sitters: again the stories are correct although I have changed a few details to preserve their anonymity. Some of my friends who are named in a particular chapter have read its contents and given their consent to have the text published.

Nanny... From This World to the Next

When I moved into a new flat with my two small children I wondered who would be my next door neighbour. We didn't have long to wait. One week later a minute elderly lady with grey hair and bright blue eyes arrived. She looked elegant with her pearl necklace, twin set and pleated skirt. A white haired man accompanied her.

The front door was wide open, the hall cluttered with crates, boxes and a rolled up carpet. They both seemed very tired. Putting down a tray with two cups and saucers and a plateful of biscuits on a chair I greeted them:

- *"Hi! I am Muriel. Welcome! Hope you will be happy here. Would you like a cup of tea?"*

My new neighbour smiled with gratitude:

- *"Well, I dare say, that is most kind of you. May I present my brother?"*

She spoke like the Queen, with gracious dignity. Smiling, I shook hands with her brother, a charming gentleman with the same twinkling blue eyes. (Perhaps I should have curtseyed!)

Later on I was to discover that the elderly lady was a retired nanny. She had looked after aristocratic children from birth to the age of seven when they were packed off to boarding school. She reminded me of a female version of Robert Donat in the film "Good-bye Mr Chips".

In due course we became good friends, a bond that would last twenty years. From time to time, she would invite me in for tea. On those occasions she would reminisce:

- *"We sailed to the Continent on a splendid yacht. I had great difficulty keeping an eye on my charges because I felt sea-sick and had to remain on deck. Imagine my surprise when, at lunchtime, the butler spread out a lace tablecloth on a small table just for me. He then served me a wonderful meal. Why, I even had a glass of Champagne!"*

Another time she mentioned casually:

- *"The children went to Buckingham Palace for tea and played with little Prince Charles and Princess Anne."*

So now, for the first time, Nanny had a place of her own - and she was thrilled! She'd never had to do a thing for herself before so housework and basic cookery became a new challenge. She soon found out that, on her pension, fish fingers were better value than smoked salmon. Nevertheless, she would always lay her small table with a linen tablecloth, silver cutlery and a white napkin in its ring before eating the couple of fish fingers and one tiny Jersey potato. Mealtimes were punctual, if unimaginative, while she watched the News on television.

It was great knowing my sons were safe with Nanny just across the landing. On Sundays I would give her a piece of homemade cake and a glass of wine which she accepted graciously. She would always be interested and enthusiastic at our minor achievements. At 86 my neighbour weighed four stone and never had a serious illness in her life.

Suddenly the old lady started to lose weight. I arranged for her to have meals-on-wheels but she just sat there, huddled up in her fireside chair, looking wan and pale:

- *"I can't eat. The smell of food makes me feel sick."*

- *"Never mind, I'll call the doctor again. Now don't worry about anything, Nanny. Try and eat just a little."*

She had shrunk to the size of a doll. The doctor arranged for her to go into hospital for the first operation of her life. (She had cancer but no one told her). Much to my surprise she fought bravely and returned with renewed vitality.

- *"It's so good to be back!"* she smiled. Over the following months I carried on looking after her. She was so appreciative and undemanding. But then her condition started to deteriorate.

Finally, when my friend couldn't stand on her feet anymore, it was time for her to go into a hospice. When the ambulance drew up, neighbours came out and hugged her:

- *"Good-bye, Nanny dear. The best of luck! See you soon."*

But they all knew it was the end. She lasted another five days. The hospice staff loved her and gave her V.I.P. treatment. When I visited her a nurse would be at her bedside holding her hand while another one stroked her hair. The situation was so touching: at the close of her life Nanny was being treated with great love and care.

My friend went into a deep sleep. But on the last day, at lunchtime she opened her eyes, recognised me and tried to smile. At about 6.30 pm one of the nurses phoned to say that Nanny's breathing was faster:

- *"Would you like to come?"*

Rushing to her bedside I realised that the old lady would not last much longer. Even in death she looked like a cute little doll. I asked the nurse:

- *"How long will it be?"*

- *"Perhaps 24 hours."*

Reluctantly I left because I had to attend my weekly circle (clairvoyance classes) at 8 o' clock. That evening my friends and I sat meditating in a subdued light. The atmosphere was quiet and peaceful. At about 9.30 p.m. one person said:

- *"I think your little neighbour is on her way out now."*

Her words made me open my eyes. Startled, I saw a bright light across the room to my left. In the silence, I watched... Everyone else had their eyes shut as they carried on meditating. Suddenly, Nanny appeared inside that glow looking around her hesitantly.

SHE HAD TWO HEADS!

Transfixed, I waited...

SHE WAS TRYING TO GET OUT OF HER BODY!

Mentally I encouraged her:

- *"Come on, Nanny. You can do it! Try a bit harder!"*

It was amazing watching her struggling, finally stepping out of her old body, discarding it like a worn out overcoat.

In front of her a large spiral of light was appearing, the size of a whale's skeleton, going right up to the other end of the room. There seemed to be a hole in the ceiling because I could see the tunnel going way beyond it. At the top her sister, who had died previously, was floating horizontally, her arms outstretched.

Nanny stood at the foot of the spiral, unsure of herself, one finger on her lips, as she looked up.

- "*Come on, Nanny, UP YOU GO! Your body is strong again. Trust me... YOU CAN DO IT! I have never let you down yet!*" I urged, mentally pushing her forward.

One minute my friend just stood there, bewildered, and the next, after one last glimpse in my direction, she jumped into the spiral and was catapulted to the top where she landed in her sister's arms. They hugged each other joyfully in the bright, flashing light.

And then it was all over. Nanny, her sister and the tunnel had vanished.

Another friend, her eyes still shut, commented:

 - "*Contact has been made. Does this make sense to you, Muriel?*"

- "*Oh, yes, it does indeed!*" I answered happily.

At 10.30 p.m. I returned home. There was a message on the answering machine asking me to phone the hospice. When I called, a nurse broke the news gently to me:

- "*I am so sorry... don't be too upset... your friend has died.*"

- "*At what time?*" I asked.

- "*At 9.15 this evening.*"

It all fitted. Nanny had passed at 9.15. She knew I was a medium and had come to me for help trusting that I would be able to guide her safely into the next world. And I had managed to do just that. It was an incredibly moving experience, one I shall never forget...

Chapter Two

The Early Years

My parents lived in Belgium before the war. In 1940, as Father had a British passport, he, my mother and elder sister Sonia (then aged 3) had to flee from the advancing German Army as did other British citizens who would otherwise have been arrested.

They packed a suitcase and took the train to Ostend but the port was already overflowing with refugees and every night German aeroplanes were bombing the town. So they travelled to Bordeaux in France hoping to board a ferry for Dover.
However, the only two boats leaving for England were already full. (One of them was to sink at sea the next day so it's just as well they missed the last boat). Those must have been harrowing times.

Seeing the plight of all these helpless stranded civilians, the skippers of two small Dutch fishing vessels decided, out of kindness, to risk crossing the Channel at night although they were unarmed and had no mine detectors. In the ensuing general panic people were pushing and screaming to get on board.

So that is how my parents finally made it to Folkestone on an overloaded little fishing boat with the Germans bombing overhead and - unbeknown to them - a U-boat trying to torpedo them from underneath. They were redirected to Nottingham where I was born during an air raid.

The sirens were blaring; at the hospital people were rushing for the Anderson shelters while my mother bravely remained in the Delivery Room to give birth to a second daughter. At this stage she was probably past caring about events outside. The doctor, a middle aged, cool Anglo-Saxon was whistling unconcernedly. And so it happened that while thousands were dying that night I was preparing to enter this world. It all happened long ago yet I distinctly remember so many details of our life in Nottingham. We lived in a house on the outskirts of the town, the only one with a crenellated privet hedge, resembling green fortifications. (Maybe subconsciously my parents thought it would protect them from the bombs.)

I was born in Nottingham during an air raid. Notwithstanding the war, my sister Sonia and I were happy. We had a large garden to play in. In winter the snow lay thick on the ground. Above: Muriel. Below: Muriel (on left) and Sonia.

In Autumn we would go blackberry picking in Sherwood Forest - an impressively eerie place to a toddler. Memories come flooding back of a clearing full of foxgloves with golden rays of sunlight filtering silently through the trees. At the edge of the forest sandbags were heaped up alongside the road and a platoon of soldiers could be seen marching up and down, their footsteps echoing in the distance.

We played happily outside in the snow in Winter. In places it was so thick I could have disappeared completely within its mantle. Mum would call us in for tea served in front of an open fire. Our noses were red and our fingers frozen: we were healthy, hungry kids. Food was rationed although we did not realise it. No child was fussy in those days: "Ooh, sweets..." We loved them all but they were seldom available.

Dad would come home late, very tired. He was employed at the Raleigh Industries Bicycle Factory which, during the war, was manufacturing arms. He worked his way up to Chief Inspector of Armaments and we were proud of him. From time to time my father would bring home small surprise treats. One night we were thrilled to see two small mauve mice dolls - one peeping out of each of his side pockets. A kind factory lady had made them out of scrap material. Mother exclaimed: "Mauve mice! Honestly, Frank, whatever next"... No other toy ever delighted us so much.

We went for walks in Sherwood Forest, a lovely eerie place. I remember sandbags piled alongside the road and platoons of soldiers marching by. From left to right: Sister Sonia, self and our father.

In 1946 my parent returned to Belgium where we were welcomed by my grandparents. Their 18th century house, built on top of a medieval graveyard, was pleasantly spooky. I am at the front left with my sister Sonia on the right. Second row from left to right: my mother and aunt. Third row: Grandad and Grandma.

As a small child I remember telling my mother about a previous life: "A long time ago I was a grown up lady. I spoke another language, had black hair, wore a long dress and rode on an animal's back. The sun was intense, and the weather very hot" but Mum would answer: "Don't talk such nonsense, come and have your lunch." There was no television and very little cinema so how could a small child invent such a story?

Another vivid memory is a recurring nightmare which I have had from the age of two right into adulthood. I was onboard a ship in a howling gale. Sheets of rain were lashing down relentlessly on the vessel as it tossed from side to side, creaking and groaning in the wind. Suddenly there was a deafening sound and I watched with horror as waves came gushing down the lower deck towards me. My heart was pounding as, terrified and soaking wet I jumped up and ran away from the oncoming surge. Still the water was pursuing me. Barefoot, I climbed up a ladder and on deck. The wind was howling in the night and I clung to a rope.

Then it all happened at once: a horrible noise of wooden planks being wrenched apart pierced the darkness and then the ship slowly keeled over on its side. At the same time a giant wave swept me up, throwing me overboard into the foaming waves below. There was a lot of screaming going on but I was paralysed with fear, in a daze, swallowing salty water and choking to death. Then nothing. Total oblivion.

Even today this memory makes me break out in a cold sweat. For years the same nightmare returned to plague me until I met Bill, a medium friend.

He said: "Why, Muriel, you were reliving a previous incarnation!"

- "Really?"

- "Now go home. Get a pen and paper and write down all the events as you remember them. In so doing you will relive the whole ghastly story which won't be pleasant but in so doing you will clear it once and for all from your mind".

How right he was! I wrote the whole episode down feeling quite sick as the details came back to life. But after that the nightmare never recurred.

Needless to say no one would get me near a swimming pool. Only last year I decided it was time to "face the enemy" and so I started attending swimming classes. Conquering the fear of water was no easy matter. It took months before I would let go of the sides. Today I can swim. Twice a week I push myself to practise otherwise I would lose my nerve and never go again. Looking at all that stretch of water still makes me feel anxious. Watching the toddlers jumping in gleefully is amazing.

When I was a child my mother could not understand why I had this vivid dream. She would make a pot of herbal tea and say:

- "Don't worry. You have probably eaten something that has given you indigestion". (She had never heard of Reincarnation.)

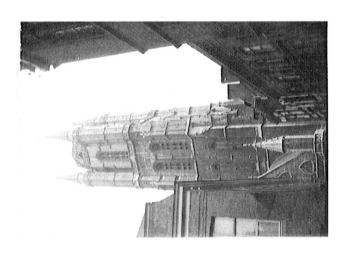

After the war, Ghent was an austere place, not the beautiful tourist town it is today. Here are a couple of pictures from the neighbourhood; no gardens, no trees. We did miss Nottingham and all its greenery.

My nightmare had started well before I ever stepped onto a boat for the first time. This event happened after the war when my parents decided to return to Belgium at Christmas. In those days the ferry was not equipped with stabilisers and the crossing took hours in bad weather. Most of the passengers were sick all over the place. Dad urged me: "Have something to eat: it will line your stomach". (You must be joking!) I looked at the man seated at the next table tucking into a hearty lunch... and the next minute he turned very pale and rushed out of the saloon.

At the time I was 5 years old - and off to discover a new world. The outline of Ostend came slowly in sight: it was pouring with rain and I shivered. We were welcomed with open arms by my father's parents with whom we stayed for a few months. They lived in a large 18th century house in the centre of Ghent. My grandmother was a delightful lady. I looked up into her smiling blue eyes and decided that yes, we'd get on fine. And we did. Right from the word 'Go'. She wore her white hair in a bun and had little round metal framed glasses. Gran was always smartly dressed in a blue suit for best with matching hat and gloves. A fox fur was usually curled around her neck. The poor thing seemed eternally fast asleep - which it was.

My Grandmother was Swiss and I would often hear her yodelling when she was homesick for her mountains. She adored her family and gave me great accounts of all their achievements - slightly embellished over the years:

- "My two daughters were SO elegant! The whole town of Ghent admired them". (Why not the whole of Flanders, or while she was at it: the whole of Belgium!)

Rationing finally came to an end and life improved greatly. Gran organised memorable Christmas parties for the family.

But, as we arrived in the aftermath of war, what a contrast with Nottingham! We were used to playing outside in a big garden backing onto playing fields, tree lined roads, Sherwood Forest... and here we lived in a terraced house of enormous proportions but not a bit of greenery in sight. Life seemed to have turned into a black-and-white film. The place was spooky, built on top of a medieval graveyard surrounding an old gothic church at the rear. Grandfather imported spare parts of bicycles and the whole groundfloor was taken up by his trade.

Often I was aware of the presence of people dressed in medieval costume going about their business in the house... but of course no one would have believed me so I kept my mouth shut on the subject, fearing ridicule more than ghosts. The

The author aged eighteen in front of the restored house with Grandma waving from the first floor.

basement, where bicycle tyres were stored, had vaulted ceilings and pillars resembling a crypt. One room still contained the ghostly vestiges of a kitchen with Delft tiles on the walls, and an ancient stone sink. I felt that somewhere a blocked up passageway led to the church. Unseen people followed me around, up and down the large oak staircase. The walls echoed stories of centuries ago. If only there had been a way of communicating...

One of the nastiest places I have ever visited in all its splendid glory is the Castle of Ghent. Today it has been restored and looks as good as new. You'd expect the Counts of Flanders to come riding out on the drawbridge at any moment. History is so close you can easily step back in time.

Now the Tower of London with all its gruesome past cannot compete, from a medium's point of view, because millions of tourists have trampled through its rooms removing the psychic atmosphere - although I am sure the presences return to haunt the place at night once the last visitors have left.

In Ghent there are fewer tourists and as a result the eeriness is preserved. Right at the top of the castle stands a genuine, well used gallows and when you peep over the walls you can still see the large hooks where corpses would hang until they rotted away. On the first floor a Torture Chamber boasts an incredible variety of grizzly instruments with lots of explanations written above just in case you miss anything.

A few years ago I returned to the Castle with my son Nathan then still a young boy. It was a grey, chilly Winter morning which made the place even more forbidding. There was not a tourist in sight. Winding our way up the well worn steps to the tower we were both aware of shadows fighting a battle up and down the stairs with echoes of swords clashing and arrows flying all around us.

Nathan whispered: "You go first, Mum and I'll hang on to you".

At last, relieved to reach the top, with the wind blowing in our faces we stood next to the gallows and admired a great view of the old city shrouded in mist and drizzle. I was determined not to let go of Nathan's hand because he could easily have fallen through one of the loop-holes.

Then we slowly walked all the way down again and into the courtyard where heavy oak doors led into the dungeons.

- "Shall we go and have a look, Mum?"

View from the Counts of Flanders' Castle, Ghent with my son Nathan as a young boy on the ramparts. One of the most gruesome haunted places I have ever visited. In the Torture Chamber well-used instruments of torture are on display.

In the dungeons, I was aware of ghostly prisoners lying in chains. Across five hundred years of history, they were asking me reproachfully: "And what are you going to do to help us?". As I gazed silently, my son Nathan (who was very young at the time) suddenly pointed across the room: "Look Mum, those prisoners are staring at us...".

24

- *"If you are quite sure".*

The minute we walked down those stairs... we were instantly swallowed up in time. The freshly scrubbed stones were now covered with matted straw. Rats scurried around... The stench was overpowering. In a state of shock I saw the ghosts of prisoners in chains lying down in the filth, some groaning and others screaming.

Unbelievable! Their spirits must have remained in that dungeon for at least 400 years. Suddenly, a hush... and all those tormented faces turned around and stared at my son and I.

Nathan gasped, tugging at my sleeve:
- *"Mum, can you see them... over there... all those prisoners. They are looking at ME!"*

- *"No, they are looking at both of us asking if we are going to help them".*

But what could I do for such a crowd of lost souls all demanding individual attention? I felt so sorry and helpless as I frantically tried to visualise a lamp illuminating the whole prison from floor to ceiling - but it was like lighting a tiny matchstick in a large cave. Concentrating even more I asked for them to be shown the path to the Next World - but it seemed such a hopeless task, they were too many.

The convicts kept looking up reproachfully, their feverish eyes following us around across centuries of History. They were able to see Nathan and I - two people they could at last communicate with in their infinite dark void. No, it was not imagination, nor was I merely picking up the gloomy atmosphere: these souls were actually there - men who believed they were still living in the Middle Ages.

Their thoughts came floating across, loud and clear:

- *" Please get us out of this nightmare!"*

How could I go to the local church and tell the priest:"The ghosts of the Castle wish you to hold a Requiem Mass for them".

He would have taken one step back and eyed me up and down suspiciously thinking I was mad. And who can blame him?

Now an adult, Nathan's drawing has captured the eerieness of Counts of Flanders' Castle, Ghent.

How many people in that predominantly Roman Catholic town would have taken me seriously?

So this is the place I arrived to as a child in 1946: Ghent, once the centre of Charles V's Spanish Court, a prosperous medieval town, resplendent with History under the shadow of the Inquisition, whose presence (to a sensitive) - apart from the recent German occupation - is still engraved in the walls.

Across the road from my grandparent's place, half demolished houses, rubble and barbed wire did nothing to lift our spirits. I could see a pub to the right. It was named "In the Hope of Freedom". Food was usually awful - not poor Grandma's fault - there was very little to eat. How does one make an omelette for six with one single egg? (Add flour, of course, sifting it first to remove any creepy crawlies, add water and powdered milk... then shut your eyes and think of Belgium).

Third rate coal in the huge dining-room chimney generated more smoke than heat. And there my grandparents and the proverbial Great-Aunt Louise sat in the evenings, well wrapped up while they played cards. From the elaborate wrought iron chandelier one single bulb threw a dim light upon the room. Occasionally the sound of opera would crackle from the radio, its music floating up to the lofty ceiling.

Mum, whose father was an orchestra conductor at the Opera, hated the stuff. Upon hearing the soprano she'd exclaim:

- "Oh! Oh! How she screeches. The woman is being strangled! Why don't they just finish her off and then maybe we'll have a bit of peace and quiet".

Everyone was in the same boat at the time, picking up the pieces after the devastation of war. Ghent was a scarred, depressing place, not the beautiful, sparkling, lively town full of flowers and cafes it is today. Dampness emerged from the canals enveloping the city in a ghostly shroud of mist. All I could see were miles of dull, terraced houses with their paint peeling off, damaged, musty churches and bomb sites.

After six months my sister and I we were pale and I became asthmatic. Mother had this money saving idea of dressing us both in battleship grey - a colour I hated and still do. But children will always find ways of amusing themselves. In that huge house (I once counted 65 doors) it was great fun playing hide-and-seek with our cousins... or we would spy on the neighbours across the road. In a basement a woman could be seen teaching ballet to young girls and in another

My mother in front of her family home in Marsh Street. She had always felt uneasy in that house and sunsequently learnt that it had been built on a gallows site. (In the attic, the next owner, a Scottish medium, wrote reams of strange gothic script, dictated to him by a restless spirit.)

men were practising jiu-jitsu - a novelty at the time - and highly entertaining to us kids. We would wonder at the G.P. taking his pet fox out on a lead when he went shopping (Yes, a fox - not a dog!). And then it was time to start school and we put England at the back of our minds but I promised myself to return one day.

So, all in all, my upbringing was not orientated towards the supernatural. Mum was fairly psychic herself but would tend to make fun of my own sensitivity. Dad was definitely not receptive to atmospheres. He could have slept quite peacefully in a haunted castle: "You heard chains rattling in the night? Of course, everything is old and rusty, what do you expect... The door was slamming? Must be a draught... Footsteps? Never heard a thing - probably a mouse". Not that he didn't believe in ghosts - he simply was not on their wavelength and would usually find a logical explanation to most problems. Father trusted in God so why would spirits harm him anyway? He'd probably have sold them a bicycle! However, there was one ghost story which shook him to the core because he was directly involved.

The House in Marsh Street

My mother was brought up in a large old house in Ghent which her parents had inherited from two great aunts. The front was painted white; dark green shutters on either side of the tall windows were closed at night, guarding its secrets.

As a young woman Mum felt uneasy in that house. She kept looking over her shoulder thinking that someone was watching her. Not only had her aunts died there but the whole atmosphere was cold, oppressive and forbidding. Neither flower pots, bright carpets nor cheerful curtains made any difference: the place remained gloomy. Homemade jams, preserves, pickles and other goodies were stored in the cellar in neat rows. Mum shuddered at the thought of going down those stairs, imagining that people were buried underneath the floorboards. But the worst room was the attic where she felt a chilling, silent presence observing her. Light filtering in through the small dormer window only added gloom to the dancing shadows. Later on the family moved to a cheerful, sunny house.

In the early 1930's my parents met at a ball and fell in love. As was customary they courted for several years before getting married. At the time, Mum was a student in Fine Arts, leading a busy life. Besides helping his father in the Bicycle business Dad was also a translator. He spoke six languages fluently and several dialects. Mum called him her Walking Encyclopedia.

My father also loved animals. I once watched him stroke a puma as it lay on its back, purring contentedly. He just had to talk to a cow over a fence and immediately all its mates would come along to inspect him hoping to be patted on the head too.

Out of the blue, Dad received a letter from the British Consul: would he be interested in translating a text of a confidential nature? Not at all intrigued by what was after all just another job, Frank arrived at his appointment a few days later.

The Consul welcomed him and they had a pleasant conversation over a cup of tea. Suddenly the man came to the point. Smiling in a strange way he handed Dad a thick file with the comment: "See what you make of this!" Frank picked up the document and, flicking through the manuscript he whistled in amazement: "I say, old chap, this scrawl looks like medieval Flemish or something. 'Fraid I can't make head or tail out of it either".

But here was a challenge which Dad could not resist. He took the papers home to his Swiss mother and together they pored over their contents. Grandma soon realised that the text was not written in Flemish at all but in medieval German. Here and there she could make out a few words of the Gothic writing. So my father went to the Reference Library in Brussels where he spent many hours poring over specialised dictionaries before he could even begin to decipher the text.

Slowly a strange story started to unfold. It was a statement written by a young man who had been wrongly accused of raping his girl-friend. The punishment for this crime was hanging. A jealous rival to the girl's affections had accused him of assaulting her. There followed a lengthy description of the trial. As Suitor No 2 was more influential the judge believed him ordering the other's execution. Now some 600 years later Admirer No 1 wished to state that although he had met his sweetheart secretly one evening, he had never slept with her. His tormented spirit would only find peace once his name had been cleared. Well, he must have had lots of patience waiting for my father, one of the most unpsychic people in the world, to help him.

What still puzzles me is how he expected his innocence to be proclaimed all those centuries later? Surely, he'd left it a bit late! The whole story left Frank baffled and uneasy, to say the least. With relief he returned the finished translation together with the original manuscript to the Consul. Thank goodness, that was over! What on earth had he let himself in for? Never again! He wondered how this weird story in medieval German of a Flemish trial had come

30

into the hands of the British Consul. But the Envoy was evidently pleased patting both himself and my father on the back for a job well done. "Would you like to meet the man who submitted the original papers?" he asked. Dad hesitated before answering: *"Okay, why not?"* The Consul continued: *"Would you deliver them? Actually, the man is Scottish..."*
He then scribbled the address on a piece of paper. Frank couldn't believe his eyes: it was his fiancee's previous home.

"In for a penny, in for a pound" thought he as, a few days later, he boldly rang the bell and waited while the sound echoed eerily through the hall. After a few minutes the front door opened and an elderly white haired man peered at my father: *"Aye, I was expecting ye... Do come in"*. The chap looked pale, obviously in a state of shock. (Worse than an opera, this). *"I nie ken yer name"* (or words to that effect) *"but this house holds good memories for ye"*.

*"That's righ*t", said Frank, *"my fiancee lived here"*.

"Do sit down and let me explain. I am a medium and was guided to buy this house because it is haunted and I can be of help.
The whole place is eerie but the psychic atmosphere is at its strongest in the attic where I felt inspired to bring a pen and paper. The minute I sat down my hand seemed to have a will of its own, covering page after page of this Gothic writing... can't understand a word of it though. However, I was told not to worry and just carry on. A man who had happy links with this house would be sent to translate the manuscript... So here you are and my task is now finished."

Six months later, my father received a telephone call from the Consul: *"Do you remember that Scottish chap with the manuscript? Thought you'd be interested to know that he has just died of a heart attack"*.

It is only later that we discovered that the house was built on marshland on the site of a Medieval gibbet. Many convicts would have been hanged there... and when their bodies decomposed they were simply discarded into the marshes. So Mother was right after all: many people had indeed been buried under the floorboards in the cellar, just beneath the pickles and jams. The house still stands there today as forbidding as ever, wooden shutters concealing its secrets. I hope the present owners have sweet dreams at night.

But, going back to my story, we moved to a pleasant flat on the outskirts of Ghent and again my poor father had to kill himself working to send us to one of the best schools in town. Mum liked the area much better too. I often visited my grandparents on my way home from school. Gran was always delighted to see me. She would produce homemade apple pie and ask, smiling: "Now tell me what you've been doing today". No story was too trivial: she would listen with great interest. My walk took me through the town park where I would pick up chestnuts for her, storing them inside my white gloves, (by then they had turned a nasty off-white).

On one occasion I gave Gran a bunch of pretty weeds. She was thrilled: "Why, Muriel, how kind of you, they are beautiful!" She arranged the flowers in a crystal vase which she put in the place of honour in the middle of the dining-room table on top of a white lace doiley. No flowers could have pleased her more. Dad travelled all over Belgium selling spare parts of bicycles to retail shops. At the time few people had cars. Bicycles were fashionable. Advertisements showed pretty young women cyclists holding a bottle of Coca-Cola to their lips and Father was very pleased with the free publicity. Everywhere he was welcomed as "Uncle Frank" and the customer's wife would immediately produce a plateful of food - whether he was hungry or not. Mum would often accompany him on his trips.

One Winter evening it was pouring with rain and my father saw two women running for the tram, just missing it. As they stood there dripping with rain, Dad, the perfect gentleman, stopped his car, opened the rear door and offered them a lift. (This was before the days of rapes and assaults). The two women were very grateful for his assistance, so grateful in fact that when he dropped them off, they invited him in. It was only then that he realised their destination was a brothel and his passengers were two prostitutes. He laughed and said kindly: "Thanks for the offer but I already have all the comforts I need at home. There is nothing you can offer me my wife doesn't have too - and it's plentiful".

He cheerfully related the story to my mother and suddenly stopped: "Oh, dear. A thought has just occurred. Supposing I had been killed in an accident with those two women, the local press would have reported: 'Businessman Frank Renard found dead in car with two prostitutes'... what would you have thought of me?"

Mum replied without hesitation: "Oh, simply that it was pouring with rain and you gave a lift to two prostitutes". That was the kind of man my father was. Mum trusted him implicitly.

During the school holidays my parents would invariably drive to Switzerland along the Rhine and through the Black Forest. This annual event took place in July. They would always stop at the same hotels, restaurants and coffee shops. Dad maintained that the fresh air would do us all good. In Switzerland I dreaded the hairpin bends in the passes when I would be jolted left and right in the stifling Summer heat. My stomach would churn and my face turn grey as I tried to cope with both nausea and asthma. It was all such an effort. (However, as I grew up, the asthma left and life became more pleasant.)

The Alps were enchanting. I loved the wild flowers, the cold, clear streams and the silence... oh, that wonderful stillness... broken by the occasional tinkling of distant cow bells... I could almost hear the mountain breathing, calling me softly. The view was magnificent, the peace supreme... an incredible spiritual experience. Nature was so close that I became as one with the mountain and ceased to exist as an individual. If death was anything like that... there was nothing to fear. Looking back it seems that my life had already been mapped out...

Chapter Three

Mediumship? Not At All What I Expected!

Like all mediums I started off with lofty ideas: clairvoyance would always flow, sitters would go home feeling uplifted and comforted... But things did not work out that way at all. Many came for anything but clairvoyance.

My first client arrived around ll a.m. on a Monday morning. With apprehension I heard the doorbell ringing. (Oh, dear! Would she be pleased with her reading?) A well to-do middle aged woman floated in, in a cloud of expensive perfume. Her clothes were well cut, her jewellery sparkling.

Nothing had prepared me for this kind of clairvoyance. I began telling her about her grandmother who had died. No, that was not what she was interested in: she was bored with her workaholic husband (but obviously not with his money) and was thinking of divorcing him provided I could guarantee that her lover would leave his wife and children for her if she did so. This person stayed with me all afternoon - 3_ hours - at the end of which she was happy with her reading and I was cross-eyed with exhaustion. (I also provided cheese sandwiches and several cups of coffee while she told me her life story in great detail).

Upon leaving she smiled and said: "I feel much better now, thanks. By the way: how much do I owe you?"

Muggins replied: "*It's entirely up to you*".

She gave me £l and drove away in her new Mercedes car.

It seems people were attracted to my gullibility like a magnet.

The following day I did not fare much better. After doing my best to bring to my client messages of support from her loved ones in the Spirit World, she snapped: "Just cut out all that trash, will you. Tell me if my son is going to divorce that bitch he is with... and can you cast a spell to get rid of her?" At that moment in time I started to feel sorry for the daughter-in-law. Needless to say my client was disappointed with her reading as I gently suggested that she should allow the couple to sort their problems out alone. (Reluctantly, she gave me 50P. I was in business!)

Late that night another woman telephoned. Her voice was soft, slow and depressed:

- *"Muriel, you are a medium aren't you?"*

- *"Yes, can I help you?"*

- *"My dear husband has died of cancer and I am so depressed"*... (Here her voice trailed off.)

- *"Are you still there? Yes? I am so sorry. Would you like to talk about it..."* (The poor woman... My heart went out to her. It did not matter that she had just got me out of bed).

- "Can you link in with your spirit guides and get me a message from him or any other relative?..."

- *"Afraid I find it almost impossible to do clairvoyance on the phone. Can't you come and see me?"*

(Change of voice. Much more authoritative): "But you ARE clairvoyant, YES or NO?"

Still a new recruit to this game I replied apologetically:

- *"I don't seem to be gifted that way"*. (How stupid I was, not having cottoned onto the fact that she was trying to get a free reading).

- *"Give me a message AT ONCE, woman!"*

By now she was enraged, her whimpering voice gone as she screamed obscenities down the phone:

- *"AAARRGGHHH! Call yourself a bloody medium....etc. etc.* (not repeatable) - and she slammed the receiver down.

Here is a variation on the same theme - this time the speaker is a man:

- *"My wife has just died... I am so depressed and feel like ending it all. Muriel, can you just talk to me..."*

- *"Oh, I am so sorry. You will see her again one day... It's not the end..."* Over the next few minutes I tried my best to give him courage.

When I had run out of ideas a silence followed...

- *"Are you still there, sir?"*

(He whispers): *"Aahh... I do feel better now, thank you for helping me....."*

Then realisation dawned on me: he had been masturbating all the time!

Now I recognise the symptoms very quickly: the slow, slurred voice, barely audible .. and I ask outright: *"Are you masturbating because if you are you are wasting my time. Try another mug. Good-bye!"* (Hope 'it' shrivels up).

Another day a frowning, angry little man in a white raincoat stormed into my flat, sat down at the table and, producing a photograph, shouted:

- *"See this picture? The seated woman is my wife. Behind her are two men standing. Just tell me which one she is having an affair with, how much he earns, what are her chances with him and upon your evidence I shall get a divorce with you as a witness".*

Just like that! Poor woman. Married to him, no wonder she was seeking consolation elsewhere.

- *"Sorry, I can't do that".*

Furious, he got up, snapping: "You mediums are all the same. No bloody good. Totally useless - the whole lot of you".

One young lady asked on the phone: *"I am going for an exam. There are 150 questions out of which three will be asked. Can you tell me which three then I will only study them?"*

Recently the phone rang at midnight. An irate man's voice demanded:

- *"WHERE ARE MY KEYS?"*

- *"How should I know?... Where you left them, I suppose!"*

- *"Well, you are clairvoyant, aren't you?. So you SHOULD know".*

- *"You expect me to apologise? Have a good search around your home and be more tidy in future!"*

I was getting tougher by the minute and quite pleased with myself. How dare he get me out of bed and accuse me for his absent-mindedness! Why don't these people ever say "Please" and "Thank you?"

A quarter of the people who make an appointment don't turn up. So I wait and wait... Why can't they let me know? All it takes is a phone call: "Sorry, I can't make it" - especially on a Sunday when I could have gone to visit friends instead or invited people for lunch.

Reminding them is a total waste of time. The standard answers are:

- *"I forgot."*

- *"I lost your phone number."*

- *"I have just come out of the bath, DO YOU MIND!"*

- *"My boyfriend had the 'flu".*

- *"Get lost! I have better things to do than ring you!".*

- *"I was looking for a new car - much more important than you as I need it for work."*

- *"My uncle has broken his left leg and I had to rush off to hospital to see him and I also had to deliver a parcel to a friend who lives miles away...*(or a similarly ridiculous story)...

Some people deliberately give me the wrong phone number. Why they book in the first place when they have no intention of coming is anyone's guess. If I call their office I am through to Battersea Power Station, Stansted Airport, The House of Lords - where, needless to say, they are totally unknown.

If anyone can survive alone in London and be successful then he or she can survive anywhere else in the world too - especially if the person happens to be a medium!

Searching for God

But back to my childhood. When I was a little girl my parents sent me to Sunday school - whether I wanted to go or not. (Looking back I guess it must have been an excuse for them to have a lie-in and a cuddle). My teacher disliked me because I asked too many questions. Ironically, today a Sunday school teacher comes to see me for a reading when her faith falters. She asks a dozen questions on religious points that puzzle her and then leaves, feeling much happier. She would not dream of mentioning to anyone that a medium had restored her faith.

If Christianity offers all the answers then why are there so many sects? And why over the past centuries had the faithful continually tortured and killed each other in the name of Jesus? After all Christ was a Jew - he never went to church on Sundays.

So I decided to find out more and discovered that there are many pathways to the light at the top of the mountain. Jesus himself would have agreed: "In my Father's house are many mansions." (Ib 2) Everyone has a right to their opinion, however far-fetched, provided they don't bother anyone else. A fanatic is someone who thinks he is right and the rest of the world is wrong. He has every intention of imposing his views on others.

My search led me to many places of worship including the most outlandish sects. While being welcomed as a long lost sister I was often offered the same sales pitch:

- "Why accept second best when this is THE true religion. Here are our books for you to read, we hold our meetings on the following days and look forward to seeing you attending regularly."

Who will ever forget the colourful Hare Krishna trooping down Oxford Street chanting in the middle of the sales? They may look rather eccentric with their shaven heads, pony tails and painted faces but they are sincere and don't disturb anyone so good luck to them. They offered me tiny sweets and invited me to their centre but I thought no - couldn't possibly join the queue.

The synagogue was an interesting place to visit. The services are dignified affairs. Like a tourist stepping back in time I watched people dressed in black with a prayer scarf around their necks bowing as they said prayers in Hebrew. Then came lovely, hypnotic music. At the height of the service the rabbi and his helpers ceremoniously took out large scrolls which they paraded around the synagogue. The congregation left their seats to go and touch the scrolls. Everyone seemed like one big happy family. Celebrating various festivals keeps people united and gives them a sense of security and belonging. Once the scrolls had been returned to their rightful place and the service was over we were offered cake and a glass of wine.

With a smile, I listened to the conversations around me:

- "Mrs Grossman, how ist ze little one?"

- "Ach, Mrs Katz, he ist getting over den chicken-pox".

If the truth were known I was more interested in the dishy rabbi who was enthusiastically telling me all about Bar Mitzvah - a ceremony when a young man is officially admitted as an adult member of the synagogue. Nodding with interest I was actually thinking how splendid he would have looked in "The Ten Commandments" with his black beard and dark eyes. The average Jew who attends the synagogue has no esoteric knowledge.

For anyone who is seeking spirituality the Theosophical Society is well worth mentioning as are the Rosicrucians.

Then, for a change, I went on a tour of the local Hindu temple. The priest, a dignified middle aged man in a white sarong, greeted me at the door, joining his hands together in the traditional way. Not to be outdone, I returned the greeting. This seemed to amuse him for a big smile lit up his face. "Welcome to this temple, let me show you around..." I'd left my shoes outside (Yes, they were still there later on) and we both proceeded barefoot on a tour of the various colourful deities.

- "This is Ganesh, the Elephant God, he brings prosperity".

(Ganesh looked cheerful enough with a garland of fresh flowers around his neck.)

- "And here is Lord Shiva - you see, he has many arms representing the various aspects of God".

(I knew this already but he told me again anyway). In the middle of the room small offerings of coconuts, flowers, sweets, had been placed ceremoniously on the floor. "And this area is holy: here we offer Pujiah - a token of thanks for having been purified and blessed."

And so we carried on with our tour of inspection in a relaxed, friendly atmosphere as I showed interest in all the statues while the priest told me their story. (Being already well read on Hinduism I could easily follow his explanations.) At the door we parted good friends. I thanked him for his hospitality and he invited me to attend their forthcoming festival with traditional dancing. This I did a few weeks later.

The place was packed. (I wondered how they would sort out the collection of shoes left outside). Some people stood and others sat on the floor - as a rule, men and women seemed to sit separately. Mums were hugging their babies while toddlers raced around in a great family outing. I half expected them to unwrap their sandwiches and thermos flasks but gathered, that in true oriental fashion everyone would be fed at the end of the ceremony.

Above the heads and noise I could see the Indian dancers, some of them children and, judging by the enthusiastic applause, their parents were in the audience. Ladies were smiling, inviting me to sit next to them on the floor but after a while, what with so many people, bright coloured sarees, flowers and noise my head started to spin and I was glad to escape into the fresh air vowing that, next time I'd bring my sunglasses along.

Another place worth mentioning is the Thai Buddhist Temple in Wimbledon. Imagine entering an enchanting world of tranquillity where no one is in a hurry. The grounds are well kept with a large variety of plants and green bushes. If you take a walk in the garden, all of a sudden you come upon a Lily pond. It's so quiet there you expect to see fairies dancing in circle above the water (well, at least I did).

The monks, with shaven heads and saffron robes, seem to glide along silently, deep in thought. Their diet is strict: a snack for breakfast, a midday meal and then nothing else to eat until the following day. It can't be much fun in winter as they sit there shivering, clasping a mug of China tea, but they never complain. Perhaps they are thinking: I am not cold, I am not hungry, the cold does not exist". They are gentle and kind.

One young chap there - whom I mentally called 'Junior' for he looked about 16 - assured me with a big grin on his face that he was 40. (What it's like to live without stress!). I would gladly have brought him some fish and chips in the evening to fatten him up a bit, but of course, this was not allowed. My motherly instincts prevailed and I settled for offering him a pair of woollen gloves because he didn't have any.

Inside the temple a large golden statue of the Buddha seated upon a lotus flower looks down pensively. The whole room seems to reflect his serenity - one feels wonderfully peaceful...nothing is worth worrying about. Just live now. Everything in this world comes and goes: love, possessions, money, fame... like an eternal wheel... and then starts all over again so if you can give loving kindness while detaching yourself from anxiety you too will be able to smile like the Buddha. (Anyhow, the monks would do a much better job teaching Buddhism, provided you can understand their Thai pronunciation).

When I remarked to the abbot: "It's all well and good but let's swop around: "I'll move in here and become so relaxed and laid back in no time while you live my life with the noise of the trains and cars outside, the bills to pay, the phone ringing constantly - and just see how serene you can remain". He laughed good-naturedly.

If someone is ill a relative will stick a small square of gold leaf onto the statue at the exact spot where the patient feels pain for he trusts that this will bring about a cure. The Buddha is full of little gold plasters so he probably never needs regilding.

The meditation had a powerful hypnotic effect on me. Looking at the Buddha, the candles and the still monks I felt swept up into space and came back much later, totally relaxed. By the way Buddha is not worshipped as a god. Tense, depressed people would benefit from meditating - it's a healthy way of recharging one's batteries.

But, returning to the subject of religion there are so many variations on the same theme it's impossible to describe them all here. Their rules are invented by man and conditioned by natural environment. Through the centuries various great masters came to earth to show the way in times of trouble - but they all preached more or less the same story: "Be good, do good, say your prayers, love and help each other" - a great message from the Spirit World. It's people who put up the barriers.

A Moslem neighbour assures me that God is masculine and that if I don't agree I shall end up in Hell in the Next World. So be it. That's my funeral. The concept of God is beyond male and female: it's spirit - a life force within all of us as well as in animals and nature. No one can put a few arms and legs together on a conveyor belt and manufacture a baby - or even the humblest flower. Well, that's my belief anyway.

A friend of mine firmly believes that God is a protestant, middle-class Englishman.

An Invitation to a Funeral

Today I ponder... Why am I invited to all the funerals, never the weddings? I seem to have a season ticket to the local cemetery. When the usher sees me he must think: "Oh, no. Not HER again!" Do I look like a grave-digger? (A middle-aged housewife in bright, cheerful clothes... Not your idea of a medium either?)

Ah, well. People remember me when they are in trouble. So I should be honoured.

A burial I shall never forget was Amy's - a neighbour. She was a delightful old lady who seemed to have been forgotten by the rest of the world. Although lonely she never complained. But where did all these long lost relatives suddenly appear from?

The Funeral

On that damp and grey autumn day the whole family
Had come in the mist for Amy's funeral, specially
In their best black clothes with wreaths of flowers, mournfully

"With love to our dear Mother, our Auntie, our Grandmother".
And now she lay to rest beneath the damp earth for cover.
Aunt Joan sighed: "My feet are killing me, I'm glad it's over".

Uncle Bob urged: "Must leave now to reach home by nightfall".
Fay smiled at her handsome cousin: "I'll accept that lift, Paul."
Lil said: "She was old and difficult - it's a release for all".

Joan nodded: "Her savings will cover the funeral, you know.
Must get the dustmen to collect her treasures tomorrow".
Lil spoke: "Her telly could go to Aunt Maud in Hounslow".

May asked: "The sandwiches will still be fresh in their foil,
Will you all come to my place, I'll put the kettle to boil".
Father John smiled: "I could do with a cup of tea, Mrs Foyle".

In the dusk, Great Aunt Emma stood alone and did not speak.
Like her sister Amy she was old, arthritic and weak.
A pearly teardrop trickled slowly down her cheek.

She recalled Amy as the child who had played, laughed and kissed.
Her old face turned slowly towards the grave in the mist:
"Farewell, little sis...", she whispered, "how much you'll be missed".

My Friend Gordon

When I try and recall all those faces from the past there is one dear chap I shall
never forget. His name was Gordon, an elderly man I had known for a few years.
He suffered with osteoporosis. His spine and neck were paralysed, his head
flung back on his shoulders: he was condemned to stare up at the ceiling and
could neither look left nor right. Reading a book must have been practically
impossible. One hip was pinned so he could only walk dragging his leg behind
him.

The doctors shook their heads:

- *"Sorry, can't do anymore for you"*.

And yet I shall always remember him with a smile on his face. He never
complained once.

- *"Hi, sunshine, how are you today?"* he would greet me.

Gordon lived alone in a specially adapted bungalow and at times must have felt
depressed as he sat in his fireside chair, reminiscing. He still had thick black hair
(with the help of a little Grecian 2000), rosy cheeks and smiling eyes behind his
dark rimmed glasses. As a young man he must have had all the ladies after him.

Gordon was a gentle, compassionate man, always concerned with the well-being of others:

- "*How are you, today, Muriel? And the boys?*"

He drove an invalid car that gave him a certain amount of freedom and he spent his time transporting friends anywhere they wished to go locally. He never charged them a penny, buying the petrol out of his own pension. Not all the people were grateful, some complained bitterly if one day he felt too unwell to be their unpaid chauffeur.

I grew to like and admire this kindly man. As soon as I arrived he'd smile: "*Come and sit down. Now let me get you a glass of sherry and then you can tell me all about what you've been doing*".

We'd chat for hours and he always made me laugh and see the funny side of life.

Then unexpectedly a friend of his phoned:

- "*Gordon was rushed to hospital last night. He suffered a massive heart attack during the night.*"

Immediately I went to visit him. He was sitting up in bed, a large welcoming smile on his pale face:

- "*Ah, there you are, sunshine... knew you'd come*", he whispered with an effort. "*Pity I can't offer you a sherry...*"

Quietly I sat down and held his hand.

- "*Can't see you*", he complained.

So I had to stand on tiptoe in front of the bed and wave.

- "*Ah, that's better*", he said, "*still the same smile*".

Gordon was attached to a cardiac machine showing his heartbeats. The way the needle was going up and down erratically did not look very promising.

He made a terrific effort to chat away unconcernedly so I did not stay long, afraid of tiring him out.

44

As I left, he squeezed my hand: *"So glad you came, Muriel"*.

And that was the last time I saw Gordon alive. The following night he had another heart attack and passed away.

So here I was, a week later, at Gordon's funeral. My pensioned neighbour, Cyril who was also his friend, accompanied me. It was summer, the only rainy day in the middle of an otherwise warm and sunny week. We had both walked around for miles before finally locating the cemetery. By the time we reached the chapel we were soaked to the skin. Cyril's best black shoes were pinching him and squeaked as they became waterlogged:

- *"I wore these at my second wedding and they fitted perfectly"*, he sighed.

His large bunch of flowers was starting to droop. We both sat down at the rear of the chapel, my umbrella dripping onto the floor into a puddle.

Shivering, I was vaguely listening to the service. "The Lord giveth and the Lord taketh away"... The vicar was doing his best in front of an unresponsive congregation.

- *"Will you please stand and sing: 'The Lord's my Shepherd'"* he encouraged us although no one was in the mood for singing. It wasn't easy. The minister then gave a short speech during which time my mind started to wander.

All of a sudden sharp pain hit me right across the chest bringing me instantly back to reality. The effect only lasted a minute and I thought: "This is what poor Gordon must have suffered when he died".

The ache subsided and I was able to sit up again and gaze ahead... straight into Gordon's smiling face. He stood in front of me, a transparent ghost, and winked as he patted me on the head, amused at my surprise: "See, I knew about life after death, didn't I? That's why I am here so quickly". Joyfully he flexed his arms and moved his head around, then proceeded to move his legs in order to show me that he was a fit man once more. Never seen him looking so well! Delighted I thought what a privilege it is to be a medium - well worth all the years of effort to get there.

Gordon's spirit slowly faded away as the vicar reached the end of his talk. He pressed a knob and the coffin slid quietly away behind closing curtains. People were sniffing and blowing their noses as they rose to leave.

- "*Thank you for coming*" said the vicar as he dutifully shook hands with the mourners.

- "*And thank you to Gordon for coming too*", I thought.

As we left, Cyril remarked:

- "*Strange, do you know I definitely felt Gordon's presence there in the chapel. He seemed to be flexing his arms and legs as if to show me that he is fit and well now...*"

After a silence, he added: "*I shall miss my friend*"...

He shivered as he buttoned up his raincoat: "*Let's go home and have a cup of coffee*".

- "*Better make it a glass of sherry. He'd like that. I am sure I have a bottle of Amontillado left in the cupboard somewhere*".

Once more we opened our umbrellas and walked down the road in the pouring rain.

But let's return to my earlier memories when I was a young woman in my twenties...

46

Chapter Four

A New Life in London

The world was out there, calling irresistibly. Adventure! New horizons... Wait for me! With my brand new qualifications in one hand and a suitcase in the other I left for London with great hope and enthusiasm. In the early sixties young Belgians dreamed of travelling but few actually did so.

- "London, I can't believe it!" the greengrocer's wife stared in amazement. "But that's so far away!".

- "She'll come running back within a month, you'll see", said Emile, the postman.

Swinging London! Just as in the films. I was delighted at the sight of red buses, black cabs, the Changing of the Guards, traffic on the left, Piccadilly Circus and men in bowler hats, (where have they gone to, by the way: are they now an extinct species?)

Oh, the crowds! So many people. The place was prosperous and clean. There was no shortage of jobs either: teenagers begging in the streets were unheard of. Samuel Johnson apparently said that anyone who is tired of London is tired of life. The man had my full support - although he did not have to commute in the rush hour. The coffee shops of his time are still there in the Strand.

On the way to the office anything can happen: you may find yourself being interviewed by a television crew requesting your opinion on a current event... or you could bump into a famous film star (and then you wonder: "Now where have I seen her face before?).

Once I saw four stage coaches, each drawn by six horses, rattling down Piccadilly Circus in the middle of the traffic. They were packed with people in 18th century costume and, would you believe it... no one took any notice.

On one occasion I took a shortcut through an old courtyard and walked straight into the filming of a Shakespeare play. Two actors were fencing fiercely along a gallery, watched by a whole crew. The shabby old courtyard had received a fresh coating of paint and looked quite impressive for a change.

One of my favourite haunts was Speakers' Corner where everyone is allowed their say - whether others are prepared to listen or not. FREE TIBET! BAN FUR! LONG LIVE FIDEL CASTRO!.... the variety was infinite.

Every week a weary old Roman Catholic priest would be droning on and on, indifferent to constant heckling. No one was ever converted - so why did he bother?... maybe it was for his own penance.

A tramp called Harry would climb up a lamppost with a bottle of Bitter in hand - he'd take a swig, wipe his mouth in his sleeve and then start telling the crudest jokes... but very entertaining and the crowds loved him.

When people started to wander off, one of the regulars, a swarthy man with greasy black hair would stand up and shout: "There is no God!" He'd wink at me and whisper: "That always gets them going."

I shall never forget an elegant young executive in a nice blue suit and matching tie who stood up on a soap box announcing: "I am now going to give a speech on anti-poofism!" Two homosexuals immediately called out: "Rubbish! Get him out!"

Soon a dozen others arrived from nowhere and the humourous retorts sparked away, a hilarious battle of wits, spurred on by 200 onlookers: "Go on, sock him, mate!"

In the background the band of the Salvation Army were playing: "Onward, Christian Soldiers" with gusto while a withered old sandwich-man with a long white beard looked on dolefully - a perfect match to his poster: "Beware, the End is nigh!"

Beyond the park, a blur of cars, red buses, black cabs and the occasional mounted horse-guards streamed into Oxford Street. I loved it all.

After working under pressure in Belgium, with some trepidation I started my first new job in London. That morning I sat alone at a modern electric typewriter and surveyed my Victorian surroundings: dark furniture, a large marble fireplace with a coal fire, efficient green metal filing cabinets... It was all so different. Would I be able to cope?

A few minutes later a friendly middle aged lady in a grey suit walked in: "Hi, I am Anne, could you type this report?" Trying to look competent I picked up the sheets of paper and thanked her. (Oh, dear! That was a lot.) Immediately I

48

started typing at top speed wondering apprehensively if it would all be finished by the evening. Suddenly, Anne's arm was on my shoulder: "Hey... where's the hurry. Take it easy. You're not in Brussels. This is not today's load - it's your work for the whole week!" She laughed: "And don't forget to take a teabreak!" Office life in London was wonderful!

At the time, I shared a flat with two other girls. It was a lovely, airy Edwardian place in Kensington... and definitely haunted. We all felt the cold, dark shadow observing us at night: someone had probably been murdered in the master bedroom some l00 years previously, who knows... the feeling was nasty and made us shiver. Today I would be able to communicate with the ghost and send it on its way. What a strange destiny! Never thought at the time of ever becoming a medium.

Which young woman does not dream of romance? In the magazines it always happened on a Saturday morning: while Marcia is busy washing her hair, the doorbell rings. It's the hunk from across the road pressing the wrong knob by mistake. She feels awfully embarrassed with a towel wrapped around her head. However, John grins: "Let's have a drink at the local this evening". Eventually he proposes and they live happily ever after. Now why is reality so different?

In those days I was still green as spinach. I met my husband at a party. He had an engaging smile and a good education. As he didn't drink, smoke or gamble either I thought: "Can't go wrong." My uncle muttered: "I would beware of a man with so many virtues." My parents warned me: "It won't work." But I was young and in love. The relationship was a complete disaster. After the wedding things got steadily worse until they became unbearable.

A neighbour confided in me: "I am so bored with my husband. I'd give anything to spend a week-end with that gorgeous man of yours!" (She was welcome to him, lock stock and barrel.)

Standing on Chelsea Bridge I remember looking down at the dark, murky water. What a release it would be just to jump in and forget everything. As I could not swim it would soon be over. There was no coming back - not a soul in sight to stop me.

Totally dejected, tears streaming down my face, I suddenly realised I was not alone anymore. A nebulous, blue shape was standing next to me. As in a dream the distant voice of my lovely Grandmother said: "Come on, now, Muriel. Where has your old fighting spirit gone to?" "Don't do it! There are many good years left ahead. Be brave and, you'll see: one day you will be happy again." Well, I just stood there, dumfounded. My old Gran to the rescue. In her favourite blue suit. She had died six months previously. And yet in my hour of need, when I'd felt no one cared, she had managed to cross over from her world to mine. Her love had saved me from making another mistake.

The shadow slowly disintegrated... I blew my nose, sniffed and looked up at the sky: the sun was setting on the Thames in soft blues, reds and gold. At that moment suspended in time, I could have touched Heaven in all its glory. Maybe suicide was not the answer after all. So reluctantly I went back home. My marriage broke up after a few years. There I was with a baby, a toddler, no money and no roof over my head. Suddenly life had turned into one big crisis.

In true Victorian style my family decided that "her only chance is to find a widower with several children so he won't object to hers". They had even discovered this marvel: he was wealthy and had four children. (Only six small kids to look after! What a bargain!)

Unfortunately the poor chap died in a car accident before I even had the chance of meeting him. It was very kind of my relatives to be concerned. However, I decided to stand on my own two feet and stay in London.

Eventually I found a flat. My nerves were shattered, my usual selfconfidence gone - I was like a prisoner emerging from a long sentence, looking at the world outside and feeling rather lost.

Little did I realise that all these hardships were part of my spiritual unfoldment. Every medium has reached rock bottom at some stage, at which point there is only one way: UP! Suffering makes one wiser, stronger and more tolerant. Had my life been plain sailing all the way with a wonderful relationship and an easy time how would I know what unhappiness is all about? If someone comes to me today and says: "My marriage has broken up, I feel shattered" - I understand exactly and can relate to their problem - whereas otherwise I would snap impatiently: "Oh, come on, pull yourself together, it can't be that bad".

Today I am very confident: no one will ever push me in a corner again. This inner strength enables me to help others roll their sleeves up and go forward through their own crisis.

In magazines the Agony Aunt invariably advises: "If you are lonely, join a club" so was it desperation that made me decide to look for a Divorced and Separated club? I put on my best red miniskirt, opened up my old umbrella and marched off in the pouring rain determined to go and meet new people. But as I neared the club my courage started to fail. After walking for miles in the night to save the bus fare there was just enough money left for the entrance fee, but none for a drink. That's how poor I was.

The club had hired the first floor of a local pub. The nearer I got the weaker my legs seemed to grow. Finally I stood outside the entrance door shaking in the cold like a newborn lamb, my heart pounding. Loud music was blaring in the background: : "Knock three times on the ceiling if you wa-a-ant me"... Oh dear, my nerves would not let me knock on any ceiling or door.

Just as I was about to turn back and run, the glass partition opened and a strong masculine hand grabbed my arm and pulled me inside. The owner of the hand was a smiling man in a grey suit who seemed amused by my nervousness. He said: "Come on, relax. I am not going to eat you." The whole room was a blur of dancing people. The music seemed to stop suddenly while everyone turned around and stared at me. (Of course, this was all in my mind. They were having a great time.) If only that green wall would swallow me up... Help! I just stood there, rigid with fear. (It is difficult for the average person to understand how one's selfconfidence can be shattered to this extent.)

My companion touched my elbow briefly as he carried on: "I'm Jack. Here... let me introduce you to some of our members: this pretty girl in front of you is Lisa - she has two small children, a boy and a girl. And this is Michael - underneath this curly ginger mop of his he is quite a nice guy"...

Gradually I met a few of the people who were sitting down. Lisa pointed me to the cloakroom. Flicking back her blonde hair she said: "You're soaking wet, love. No wonder you're shaking. Go and hang your raincoat over there,". That, in itself was another ordeal. The Ladies' provided a safe haven. It took more courage than I could muster to emerge once again with a fixed smile on my face. A pleasant, skinny woman finally came to my rescue and led me to a chair next to hers. Gratefully I sat down trying to hide behind someone else with a blank face. A tall chap with thick black hair walked over and asked: "Hello stranger, could I have this dance?" I declined politely and he went away shrugging his shoulders.

Yet, I was brave enough to return the following week and was gradually introduced to the great D & S establishment. At least here everyone else had been hurt too. They unloaded their tales of woe as I listened patiently not realising at the time that this was already an introduction to the work I do today. What a strange world of lonely people trying to sort themselves out and start again!

The club helped me regain my self-confidence. Eventually I joined the committee, organising parties, outings and welcoming new members. Oh, the memorable get-togethers full of intrigue and gossip! One would dress up carefully for these special occasions, setting out full of hope to return home later on, slightly tipsy and even more fed up and disillusioned than before.

A sorry imitation of Marilyn Monroe nudged me: "I fancy that gorgeous Romeo over there across the room". "Yes", I answered, "And that is his girlfriend with him". She carried on: "But I am better looking! Do you think I stand a chance with him... and, tell me, how can I get rid of her?" (Try a little arsenic, perhaps? Just charming, this aspiring Marilyn...)

There were neurotic actresses out of work, ex convicts, disenchanted travelling salesmen and among that odd assortment of clashing personalities some were actually pleasant, interesting people. A member called Kate invited us all to a Halloween party in her large Victorian house. The poor woman's place was in a dreadful mess with children and dogs running around adding to the general chaos. She opened the door in a state of panic. Kate had made several pumpkin pies but forgot to put them in the oven. Her dyed blonde hair had not seen a comb for several days.

The stress proved too much for after a short while she asked all her guests to leave. Our hostess had changed into her dressing gown and was going to bed. We waved good-bye to the grinning hollowed out pumpkins, the dogs, the hamster and tiptoed out. Kate never returned to the club. Falling in love is a gamble at the best of times. Hazel, a sincere gentle person, had the misfortune of moving in with handsome Joe. He had silvery sideburns, dark sparkling eyes and distinguished features. What a catch! In fact Joe had it all planned out. He promised her the moon and opened a cafe, making Hazel do all the work while he put his feet up and took the money. At closing time, after inspecting the place to ensure that she had cleaned it thoroughly, Joe brought her back to his home where he expected to be waited upon hand and foot.

He constantly complained that Hazel was becoming slack and could not keep up the pace. No wonder his wife had left him! So eventually did the exhausted girlfriend. Joe had all the makings of a first-class pimp. Maybe he has become one today.

Another incident stands out in my mind. Walking into the club with - finally! - a new dress I felt great. It had a white short-sleeved top and a long flowery skirt. With me was James, my current boyfriend, a pleasant, intelligent man, always in a good mood.

A drab looking middle-aged woman with straight grey hair rushed up, threw her arms around him, totally ignoring me.

- "Oh, dawling", she exclaimed, "it's awfully nice to see you. We must get together soon. Do tell me when you are free".

Standing behind them, slightly amused I was totally unprepared when she hit me hard in the ribs with both her elbows while kicking my legs with her stiletto heeled shoes to push me out of the way. She carried on purring and James never noticed a thing. Such cattiness! Pauline must have been a bitter, lonely and unhappy person - I almost felt sorry for her.

All these people were so hurt and lonely - desperately looking for a perfect relationship. Her type asks me today: "Will you cast a spell for this man to love me?"... "Can you get rid of his wife?"...

We have freewill. There is no way I am going to force someone to do something against their wishes. It is against cosmic laws. (Pauline should have tried being a bit more loving herself in the first place.)

One woman simply requested: "Would you make me a talisman to eliminate all future problems for the rest of my life?"

I replied: "My dear, it that were possible I would be wearing one myself right now".

Sid, a member of the club, was a chauffeur for a wealthy Arab potentate. He announced weeks in advance that His Magnificence had condescended to honour the club with his presence. Sure enough the man arrived out of the blue. Judging by the air of expectancy and the kow-towing entourage preceding him he must have been very wealthy and influential. There was a hush as his bodyguard and half a dozen other puppets in dark suits lined up to clear the way. Then the great man himself entered in style. Much to my surprise I saw a pint sized chap with a pronounced squint in his gleaming dark eyes. His suit was immaculate and probably cost the earth. In the subdued light diamonds glittered like flashing cameras. That still did not make him likable. Here was a ruthless character used to giving orders and being obeyed at once.

Ignoring him completely I carried on a conversation with some friends. From the corner of my eye I observed him slowly glancing around the room, his eyes resting briefly upon every woman before moving on. It was like a game of Roulette... the needle moving on relentlessly while the gamblers held their breath. *"Les jeux sont faits, rien ne va plus"...* Suddenly his finger pointed at me. Was he saying: "I'll have that one for the night! Does she come gift wrapped?" Sid must have assured him that he could have the pick of the crop. It made me feel like a lobster in the fish tank of a restaurant awaiting its fate.

Soon Sid was at my side, anxiously wringing his hands: "My boss wishes to have this dance with you". "Certainly, Sid, show me the way to the Kasbah". Dutifully I followed him across the room to be introduced to Suleiman-the-Almost-Magnificent. All eyes were on me this time as the Arab bowed stiffly, clicking his heels and, grabbing my hand, we waltzed around the room. Conversations resumed. Although under 5' in height this man was obviously politically powerful. His beady little eyes were squinting lustfully down my blouse. At the end of the dance, he walked away a few paces, snapped his fingers at one of his attendants and whispered: "Book a table for two at the Savoy".

Sid, a worried look on his face, came over:

- "My boss wishes you to join him for a meal at the Savoy Hotel. He is very generous. Please go... he will treat you well".

(At what price? It was obvious that dinner was the last thing on his mind). Being chosen for the night by a prominent Oriental was amusing, but enough was enough.

- "Tell your boss I would be pleased to join him provided my boyfriend James over there can come as well".

- "Oh, no..." Sid groaned.

The poor chauffeur reluctantly conveyed the message of doom to the Arab; His Magnificence turned crimson with fury and within a matter of seconds he had marched off the premises followed by his nervous entourage. The sound of his angry footsteps still echoes in my mind...

A Strange Encounter

At the time it was impossible for me to hold down a job. I'd pay neighbours to take my sons to school and bring them back. What does one do during the holidays? Or when the neighbour announces: "Sorry, can't have them tomorrow. I am going out for the day". The few nurseries were full and I could never afford a nanny. There were no facilities for working mothers.

I did all sorts of odd jobs but found that temporary secretarial work was convenient as I could take time off. If I arrived at work a quarter of an hour late because, perhaps of a bomb scare at the station, then those fifteen minutes were deducted from my salary. Public holidays were unpaid. Every week I was anxiously waiting to hear from the agency whether they had found me a suitable vacancy for the following week.

On one occasion my employers sent me for three weeks to an office near the Strand. That Monday morning, I set off with my A to Z map of London and butterflies in my stomach. There was no difficulty in finding the address: No 6 was an austere and somewhat forbidding Edwardian building - all in height. The door was open and I walked into a dark hall with a high ceiling.

A pleasant middle aged man, with dark hair, heavy spectacles and an engaging smile, appeared: "Muriel? Hello. Do come in. Thank you for coming. We desperately need some help here. I am John, the manager. Let's go and meet the rest of the crew". We did the rounds and I shook hands with a dozen people. No one seemed harassed or under stress. They were all efficient and friendly.

The manager showed me into the front office - probably once an impressive drawing room, with its large marble chimney. "I hope you will be comfortable working with us. We're not a bad lot", he smiled. "Just call if you need anything". My desk too was from a bygone era although the typewriter seemed up-to-date. I sat down on a green leather upholstered chair, peeped at the busy street outside, and started to type. Within half an hour, feeling comfortable and relaxed, I had settled in, working at a steady pace, with a mug of coffee to speed me on my way.

From time to time someone would stop by and call: "Hello, hope you like it here" or: "What are you doing for lunch, Muriel? How about coming to the local for a salad?... Twice, that morning, while I was concentrating, someone brushed against me and when I turned around to say "Hello" the room was empty - yet each time I'd felt a cold draught.

In the room next door, Gina, a pretty, lively hippy clerk was filing documents. (She dressed in outlandish clothes just to see the staff's reaction.) On this occasion - having just returned from a trip to Calcutta - she was wearing a haphazardly draped red saree and lots of bangles, rings and necklaces. A big smile lit up her face: "Hi there, how are you getting on? Dead place, isn't it? Wish I could liven it up with some of my records! Tomorrow I'll bring my guitar along. That should wake 'em up... especially when they hear my wonderful, croaky voice!... Hey, how about another coffee?. It's eleven o'clock anyhow".

We chatted for a while and then I asked: "By the way, something strange happened a while ago. Although alone in the room at the time I definitely felt someone watching me. "Am I imagining things?" Gina laughed: , "Dear me, no. In actual fact, we all feel the cold air when our resident spooks potter about. Never believed in ghosts myself until I worked here. It certainly livens it up a bit."

That whole morning I never felt alone. It was unnerving - like being watched by an unseen audience whose presence was so real that at one stage I got up and tapped the wood panelling wondering if there might be a secret door... but no, nothing moved. Feeling rather uneasy I inspected the windows, the ceiling... and shivered. The Victorian clock on the wall slowly ticked the hours away...

Why did this place feel so cold and eerie... full of dark shadows? Thank goodness the staff were friendly. The manager popped his head through the door: "Do you know how to use the photocopying machine? Yes? That's good. They are all pretty much the same. Anyhow, could you take a few copies for me... here, it's about 100 pages. I'm off to a meeting... late already. You will find the machine downstairs - first door on your right - the switch is at the entrance. Give a shout if you want any help".

Then he was off. After finishing the letter I picked up the file and went into the hall. A winding marble staircase led up to the first, second and third floors, and down to the cellar. My heels echoed loudly in the silence, as I spiralled my way down towards two enormous pillars at the bottom, supporting a vaulted ceiling. "This must be pretty ancient", I thought, "it's just like a crypt". A heavy oak door on my right looked forbidding indeed.

By now both the silence and the musty smell were becoming oppressive. (Did I really have to go through with this?) Apprehensively, I pushed the door and it slowly creaked open, groaning loudly on its rusty hinges. What lay ahead? Dracula's chamber, maybe? With a sick feeling in my stomach I switched on the light and stepped into... a perfectly ordinary looking office with whitewashed walls. Everything was clean and tidy with fluorescent lights hanging from the vaulted ceiling. What a relief... and yet, the atmosphere felt sinister... I was finding it increasingly difficult to breathe. "Come on, Muriel old girl, no time for imagination" I told myself firmly. Ah! There was the photocopying machine in the corner - one of the latest models too. It was soon switched on and the photocopies slid on top of each other rhythmically. I hummed a tune, ignoring the goose pimples on my arms.

At the far end of the room, three stone steps led down to a large metal cage, reaching right up to the ceiling. It contained neat piles of stationery and old files. Everything went smoothly for the first five minutes as I concentrated on the work. But why did the place seem to grow colder and even more oppressive? I started to wheeze but carried on regardless. It was then that time stood still... frozen, as had become the temperature in the cellar. An icy draught was coming from the cage... a distinctive yet invisible presence slowly dragging itself towards me. It came much closer... while the cold intensified... and stood right behind my left shoulder, breathing frost down my neck. My left hand, arm and neck went numb while my right side remained reasonably warm. My heart was pounding... I was feeling weak.

Instinctively I knew that the ghost was a sad, anguished woman and that she was taking my own energy to manifest... Her husband had kept her locked up in that cage where she had languished until her death - perhaps 200 years ago. Maybe she had gone mad with grief. Had he spent her dowry on gambling and other women? Or did he simply pretend that she had disappeared? Who knows... I felt very sorry for her but as she touched me while looking over my shoulder, her presence was quite unnerving.

At the time I had no idea how to cope with ghosts. Although scared, I thought the best thing was to chat to her so I explained how the machine worked: "See, this is for copying written pages. You put the sheet in here - and out comes the copy at the right. Sorry if I am intruding but the work has to be finished. Won't be long".

By now I was suffocating, giddy and faint but carried on nevertheless wishing the copier would speed up. At last I assembled the sheets as calmly as possible and, calling: "Byebye, ghost" strolled nonchalantly towards the oak door. It protested loudly, the sound echoing behind me... Then I ran! Up the stairs, two steps at a time... gasping, choking. NEVER AGAIN! No one would ever make me go into that crypt again.

"Surely, you don't believe in ghosts!" the manager reassured me. "However", he conceded, "I do agree that the atmosphere in the cellar is unpleasant". (The dungeon, you mean!) The practical no-nonsense accountant nodded his head wistfully: "One Saturday evening I was upstairs in my office catching up with some work. I was alone in the building but distinctly felt the presence of two entities watching me intently. Not ashamed to admit this to anyone: I was petrified!"

Poor lonely ghost! Maybe she is still haunting that cellar to this day. Various staff members have felt the presence of other spirits throughout the house - it's a pity they could not all get together and have a ball. Maybe one of them is her husband.

I shall never know...

Matters were slowly improving although I was still under a lot of stress finding it difficult to relax. Bringing up two small children alone with little money and the anxiety of a divorce is no fun.

Little did I know that a new, fascinating chapter was just about to start. A chance remark would change the course of my life.

Chapter Five

Meeting With a Medium Called Bill

Marie, a neighbour, suggested out of the blue: "Muriel. You are a bundle of nerves. Why don't you pop over to Wimbledon Spiritualist Church and have some healing?. I often go there myself".

- "I beg your pardon... HEALING? ME? The whole idea makes me feel uneasy." Already I had visions of being bathed in the River Jordan while a High Priest in a white robe cried: "Hallelujah, praise the Lord. She is saved!" (Oh, no. That was certainly not my scene). However, once while shopping in that area I thought: "Why not be daring?" So I went in not knowing what to expect. According to the Agatha Christie stories mediums are elderly ladies dressed in black with a veil over their head. Would the place be dark and spooky like a mausoleum?

Walking across the porch I wondered nervously what lay ahead. Amazing... it was not at all what I expected. The walls were pale blue... with fresh flowers everywhere, some in vases and others in pots. A wonderful, peaceful feeling permeated the atmosphere. Sunlight filtered through the stained glass windows onto a lovely arrangement of daffodils on the altar.

A smiling lady came to me and asked: "Are you here for healing?"

- "Er... yes," I mumbled.

- "Do sit down in the hall. Anyone in particular you want to see?"

- "No, no one, thank you, any healer will do".

- "That's fine", she said. "By the way, my name is Connie. Would you like a cup of tea while you are waiting?. There are four other people in front of you".

Gratefully I accepted the tea. Next to me a pretty young lady with thick brown hair and a Yorkshire accent asked: "Been here before?"

- "No", I replied hesitantly.

Bill and Joan Marie, two lovely people who changed my values and my life.

Bill was born with the ability to see spirits around him. He would hold conversations with my ancestors, over my shoulder. It was amazing! Especially as everything was so accurate. It would have been impossible for him to find that kind of detailed information anywhere.

Over the years, Bill patiently taught me clairvoyance while Joan plied me with cups of tea and pieces of homemade cake.

They died within six months of each other.

- "I've been coming for a while" she continued "and my nerves are much better now. You should go and see Bill in the sanctuary. He's great... he tells you things".

When it was my turn Connie invited me to go inside the church and sit down on a stool. A middle-aged man sat on another seat in front of me and gently held my hands while a young lady in her late twenties stood behind me and put her hands on my shoulders. She smiled reassuringly: "Just shut your eyes and relax. There's nothing to worry about".

Slowly her hands became burning hot and, as she concentrated, a powerful current vibrated through my body, from head to toes. It was incredible. Then her hands rested lightly on my head, erasing all the jangled up worries from my mind after which she directed the energy to my stomach. The heat ironed out the tension and the butterflies simply flew away.

After about twenty minutes the power switched itself off. I opened my eyes and saw the young lady slowly coming out of a daze herself. On an impulse I touched her hands: they felt cool to the touch. The treatment was so relaxing I could have nodded off to sleep.

"This is absolutely amazing" I said. "By the way - how much do I owe you?"

They both laughed: "We offer our services free. There is a dish in the hall. You can put some change in if you can afford it but otherwise, don't worry. If you feel better that is payment enough. Do come again".

I went home floating on a cloud. Why, no one had preached nor tried to convert me to anything! They were friendly but not "Holier than Thou"... just ordinary people. It suited me fine.

The following week I returned determined to meet this mysterious Bill. There was a long queue waiting to see him. While sipping another cup of tea I felt myself calming down just by absorbing the peaceful atmosphere. Soon other patients started talking to me, turning the evening into a pleasant discussion. Finally my turn came to enter the sanctuary at the rear of the church: a small room, again full of flowers. Paintings and a few religious prints hung on the walls. With surprise I noticed a pastel of a North American Indian and another of a Zulu. (Later on, I was to learn that these are spirit guides).

Three women and a man welcomed me. Bill was a short, stocky Cockney in his shirtsleeves. His hair was neatly combed with a parting on the side and he wore glasses. The healer looked rather tired and harassed but a big smile lit up his face: "Hello, love! What can I do for you?... Just sit yourself down on that stool." Now when Bill gave healing the power was so strong that his hands were shaking as though they had been plugged into an electrical socket. The sensation was wonderful... one of floating up to the ceiling.

After the treatment Bill said thoughtfully: "Hmm... Going through a divorce, are you? Two little boys... I've got your Grandad here. Philip... was that his name?" (Yes!). "There's not much he didn't know about bicycles, is there?... He is saying you've had a rough time but life is slowly starting to improve. By the way, you are going to move - and one day you will be a gifted medium yourself."

Just like that! How did he know my grandfather sold bicycles? Or that I had two sons? As to the last bit... me, a medium! It was too much to take in at one go.

Every week I returned for healing and after two months felt much more relaxed and confident.

In no time I asked to learn this wonderful gift and was patiently taught. Over the years healing has proved an invaluable help with all sorts of problems. It seems to go hand-in-hand with clairvoyance. When I give a reading to a person I may suddenly feel a slight twinge say, in my left arm. So I would ask: *"Do you have problems with your arm?"* and the sitter would reply, surprised: *"Now how did you guess? Yes, it's the left one".*

Standing behind the patient I feel their aura (the energy field around the body) with the tip of my fingers without touching them and sure enough, usually know where the problem lies and whether the complaint is serious or not. A healer does not replace a doctor and is not allowed to diagnose.

Spirit give me all sorts of information. A very nice lady came to see me for a reading. Straight away I liked her because she was pleasant and level headed. Karen had a lot of problems at the time but to me they were not as important as her health. Although she looked well I felt there was something wrong with her requiring urgent attention and insisted she went to see a gynaecologist.

She looked at me incredulously: *"But I have had tests recently and all is well".*

But I was adamant: *"Then you won't lose anything by having another check-up just to please me. I feel something is not right but if you get help soon it won't be much and you will be fine".*

Reluctantly, Karen made an appointment with her G.P. only because I insisted.

This is the story as she recalls it:

"A while ago I came to see Muriel in desperation for help with family problems. I was very keen to come, looked forward to it and was not nervous at all because I did not think there was anything to fear. When Muriel opened the door I felt very welcome as though I had known her for a long time. It was a nice, calm atmosphere. She told me I had a problem with my stomach and advised me to seek medical opinion as soon as possible. She was persistent that I should go and even offered to come along with me to my G.P. I knew that perhaps there was something wrong but the doctors kept on giving different reasons or excuses as to what it was. Muriel said I should insist to see a consultant, it was my right. So I did.

The doctor did make tests but they were negative but as soon as the gynaecologist examined me she found that there was an ulcer at the neck of my womb. She took more tests and discovered it was the first stage of cancer. Within six weeks I had Laser treatment under anaesthetic which removed all the bad cells. Now I have regular tests every year. If Muriel had not persisted I would never have gone to the doctor's and insisted to see a gynaecologist - and would not be here today". Karen. (Name and address supplied).

This is only one of many instances when spirit intervened because there was a need to save that person's life. Six months later it would have been too late. I was simply passing on a message without alarming the patient and don't take any credit for it.

However, returning to those early days when I was going to see Bill for healing, on one occasion, much to my surprise, he took off his watch and handed it over to me. "Here you are, love. Hold this article in your hand and tell me what impressions you get".

Puzzled, I replied hesitantly: "Well, this is your watch. It's a man's watch. You must have had it for a while as the strap does not look new anymore".

Bill laughed and turned to another lady: "Here, bud, can you show Muriel how Psychometry works, because I haven't got the time just now with all these patients waiting".

A slim lady with short white hair smiled: "Come and sit next to me and I'll show you." Fascinated, I followed her and we sat in a corner.

"What is Psychometry?" I asked. (The vicar in my C of E upbringing never mentioned any of this).

She answered: "Well, it's a question of making an article talk to you. First of all, you ask it questions: Is this watch male or female, gentle or tough? Has it been through water or fire?... Do you get a good feeling or not? Once you can distinguish these facts you continue concentrating and more ideas will come. Don't try and reason whether they are plausible or not. Just give off whatever comes to your mind without thinking. It's a way of developing your sensitivity."

She removed a heavy gold cross and chain from around her neck and handed it over to me: "Here you are, practise on this. Take it home with you and bring it back next week. Write down all your impressions". Another amazing person! She'd never seen me before and yet she knew I would not disappear altogether with her jewellery.

So I did as she requested and the following week returned her cross with my written comments. As she read, she smiled, delighted: "Now what did I say? You've done it. I can accept most of the writing! Simple, isn't it?" (And I thought I was just making it all up! What eccentric practices in a church!)

Since then I have developed this gift and it never fails. A sitter may be smiling and chirpy but the moment I pick up her keys or say, her watch, I know straight away whether she is putting up a front or not. Past events and the owner's temperament have left an imprint on the article. When a woman is wearing a ring belonging to her grandmother then occurrences in both their lives remain on the piece of jewellery.

An article that is soft and light to the touch belongs to a gentle person. When it seems unnaturally heavy the owner is burdened down with worries. An object that feels hard and rough belongs to a difficult person - or someone who has had a hard life. When, for some unknown reason, the gadget seems very cold then perhaps its owner has died.

At first you are fantasising but with practice you will discover that your impressions are accurate. Don't analyse your thoughts. Just say whatever comes to your mind however far fetched it may seem. For example, while holding a ring you see a road leading to a bridge over a river and as you concentrate you will carry on in a dreamlike state following the article's trail through fields or streets. And the owner will exclaim: *"How interesting, you are describing the village where I was born"* - or else: *"That's the place I was driving through yesterday"*.

64

Often the spirit of the deceased person hovers around the piece of jewellery. Let's take, for instance, a necklace that would have belonged to Queen Marie-Antoinette, one she would have worn frequently. The fear and horror of her last days would still be imprinted on the object. Marie-Antoinette herself may appear to the wearer of her pearls bringing along a feeling of doom and gloom. So, under her influence, the new owner could also become deeply depressed and attract misfortune upon herself. A historical jewel may have a reputation of being cursed and no one will wear it. This is the reason behind this belief. Looking at someone's handwriting or photograph works the same way. Nonsense? Mere superstition? Not really.

You'd never guess what people have brought for me to psychometrize!

The first surprise was a small wooden box containing grey powder.

- "*My Grandad's ashes!*" the young lady announced proudly.

Ugh! No disrespect to the old man but I told her to put it straight back into her carrier bag. (This reminded me of the story of customs officers at Heathrow Airport who dipped their fingers in a similar casket and tasted its contents thinking it contained cocaine!)

One young lady produced her boyfriend's creased flowery underpants fished out of the bed that morning:

- "*That's all I could find in a hurry. Could you just hold the briefs and tell me if he is faithful?*"

Another bright spark carefully unwrapped an object in a silk scarf and - guess what! Deceased Gran's false teeth were grinning at me. (I suggested she should be allowed to speak for herself!)

And once a frumpy, prim and proper woman who was getting on in life, declared at the end of her reading:

- "*Yes, I am pleased with what you told me... but you never mentioned my boyfriend.*"

Taken aback, I looked at her straight grey hair, sensible shoes, general dowdy appearance and asked:

- "Sorry, but er... do you have his photograph? That might help."

- *"Certainly"*.

She not only produced one, but three pictures of a pot-bellied, bald headed man standing stark naked on a balcony somewhere in Switzerland with full frontal and side views of his equipment.

- *"Isn't he gorgeous? That's my Phil. Now could you hold his photographs and tell me if he is going to leave his wife for me*?"

(Oh, dear! If I were a man and had something like that, I'd hide it.)

But, I digress. Going back to the church and healing... One day Bill announced out of the blue: "I am starting a circle in September. Would you like to join, Muriel?"

- "What's a circle?" I asked, puzzled.

"Development classes, love. Let the 'little fat fellow' teach you clairvoyance - if you're interested, that is." Me! Interested? I was fascinated. (Far more exciting than the Divorced and Separated club any day.)

And so I went to Bill's house that first Friday in September. It had been a lovely, mild day and now the sun was setting in the sky behind the rooftops. My friend lived in a modest three-bedroom terraced house in South Wimbledon on a very busy road. The door was opened by his pretty wife, Joan. A decrepit dog peeped at me from behind her legs. "Oh, hello," she smiled "we're all upstairs in the spare room". So up we went and joined six other enthusiasts. The box room was used solely for clairvoyance and healing.

The course started with Bill patiently teaching us all the ins and outs of mediumship - not only how to develop the gift but also how to keep it under control. He was delighted at any progress we made. It took years of perseverance before I was any good at clairvoyance. Afterwards in their comfortable front room Joan would ply us with cups of tea and homemade cake. They both simply accepted me. It was like being adopted by a new family.

Bill was the president of Wimbledon Spiritualist Church and an electrician by trade. He was also a dreamer and an idealist. Totally loyal to his wife and friends, he would do anything for people, go out of his way for them. Anyone in a crisis could call Bill in the middle of the night and he'd quietly reassure them :

"Hang on, love. I am putting on my coat and I'll be with you in ten minutes".
Nothing was too much effort. His home was always full of people: those who
were waiting for healing or a reading, others just popping in for a chat. Friends,
neighbours, lost souls and lame ducks alike - he cared for them all. This kind
man was born clairvoyant. As a small child he saw invisible people around him
at all times. He made me feel safe: if I had a problem, no need to say anything -
Bill would look at me quizzically and give the answer there and then.

After a few months our teacher decided to make us practice clairvoyance in front
of an audience. There is nothing more frightening, in my opinion, than facing a
sea of faces when you have not prepared a text. As you stand up, all eyes are on
you, your mind goes blank, your stomach is churning - you feel absolutely sick.
It took a lot of courage not to run off the stage and give up... (or throw up). Bill
was always there helping, encouraging. Mind you, he was not a marvellous
example - being nervous himself on a rostrum.

Give Bill his slippers, his cup of tea and his fireside chair and he'd delight you
with a marvellous reading. But stand him in front of an audience and he'd feel
uneasy in his best dark green jacket and tie. As he worked he'd slowly remove
first his tie, then his jacket and finally his glasses before rolling his sleeves up -
when at last, with a sigh of relief, he'd be ready to give messages. We teased
him, offering to bring his chair along and a mug of tea to help him unwind.

This unassuming man recruited everyone's services. "You love dogs, you say?
Well can you look after old Bonzo while I am away - there's a good girl".... -
"Don't say you are 'only' a cleaner, love. It's a very useful job. Be proud of your
skills. It would be great if you'd give us a hand in the church... You can sing?
Wonderful! Would you like to perform in front of an audience?..." And the
strange thing is that people fell over to help.

Bill enrolled his friends to form a group which he called "The Silver Rose". He
organised special events in halls and Spiritualist churches all over the South of
England. Anyone who could sing, play an instrument, entertain, give a
demonstration of clairvoyance or do healing was roped in.

The evening would start off with a giggling introduction by a nervous Bill (in his
green jacket). Then one or several volunteers would play the piano or any other
musical instrument available, accompanied by whoever was willing to sing.
Perhaps someone would tell a funny story and three mediums would follow with
a demonstration of clairvoyance.

At the same time healers would be giving their services at the rear of the hall. I have never seen so many enthusiastic patients as suddenly people in the audience remembered they had a variety of aches and pains. Maybe they were genuine, or perhaps just curious. Perhaps they simply wished to stretch their legs as they tiptoed in turn towards the back of the room, but we were kept busy for hours giving healing on a conveyor belt to a large crowd.

Soon another musical interlude would follow. Then three more mediums (or the same ones if he was short of recruits) would give a further demonstration. To round off the evening Bill invited everyone to join in a sing-along of his favourite tunes - after which we'd all queue out to a wonderful spread of food. This led to very successful evenings in packed halls. I came in useful either with clairvoyance or healing. It was great training and fun at the same time. Usually a last minute crisis occurred: the soprano had tonsillitis or a medium's car had broken down on the motorway. However, the audience never noticed anything. The presenter just giggled a little more than usual.

Bill had a simple philosophy of life: "If you work for Spirit, you will never be rich but you'll always have enough. They won't protect you from worries but will always be there to hold your hand and pull you out". I listened because it made sense.

Winter came and Joan was looking forward to Christmas. She had made so many plans. On the 22nd of December she rang my bell and excitedly produced a little present wrapped up in shiny paper. The next day she had a heart attack and died at home in Bill's arms. Joan was only about 50. In a daze I remember thinking stupidly: "Now why didn't she die on Boxing Day after having opened all her presents with her family around her?"

Her poor husband was devastated. At my home he'd call every day and would often stare vacantly for ages before repeating the whole last episode over and over again. I would make him cups of tea and simply listen. All his friends rallied around him and after six months of feeling like a Zombie, he started to get back on his feet. Hesitantly he smiled: "It's not easy for me to say this, Muriel, but you've been a good friend to me". It was like being awarded a gold medal! The following week he too collapsed with a heart attack and died as suddenly as Joan.

Bill would be pleased to see me today giving messages to crowds of people in total confidence. I owe him a lot. And so do hundreds of others: he tried so hard to help them all.

Old Flo

A few years ago I was organising the Mobile Library for the Housebound in my area and that is how I came to ring her bell. After what seemed like an eternity Florence Smith came shuffling to the door, wiping her gnarled right hand on her flowery apron. The other arm hung limp. She was an old woman in her eighties, with a wrinkled, sallow face, straight white hair and clever blue eyes that now proceeded to look me up and down suspiciously:

- "And what do YOU want?"

- "Would you be interested in having library books delivered?" I asked cheerfully, forcing a smile on my face.

- "Oh, yes? And what would that cost?" she snapped.

- "Nothing... really, nothing at all."

- "Then what's the catch? Do you get paid for this?" Her eyes narrowed and she frowned, wondering why anyone would offer her something for free.

- "No, there's no catch at all. This is voluntary work I do in my spare time."

Shrugging, she nodded:

- "Oh well, I suppose you'd better come in then. Mind you wipe your feet on the mat!"

So I followed her down the hall into the cluttered sitting room. A dark oak china cabinet took pride of place near the window. It was full of souvenirs from Clacton-On-Sea, Blackpool and other popular holiday resorts (probably all made in the same factory in Hong-Kong). Gingerly I sat down on a stiff backed chair next to an ancient standard lamp with brown fringes on the shade. The settee was covered with an amazing assortment of cloths and lace doilies. Still, the effect was reasonably pleasant.

Flo sat opposite me and, somehow, we hit it off straight away. The poor woman was crippled down her left side and could not move without feeling pain. But she had a sharp tongue and a terrific sense of humour. By the time I left we were both in high spirits.

Grudgingly she remarked:

- "You're not a bad sort, really..."

Then, forgetting her feigned indifference, she leaned forward eagerly:

- "Tell me: when can you come again? How about next Tuesday?"

What had I let myself in for? So, dutifully I returned to visit Flo every week for several years and grew quite fond of the old battle-axe. She'd had a hard life, an unfaithful husband, and very little spare cash. She loved telling me her life story over and over again:

- "This woman arrived on my doorstep, shouting defiantly:

- 'Your husband and I are lovers! So what are you going to do about it?'... (Thought I'd be upset!)

- "'Fine' I replied, 'have 'im! He's all yours... couldn't care less as long as you wipe your feet on the mat before you come in. I've just cleaned the floor.' "

Chuckling she added:

- "You should have seen her face, ha-ha!"

Flo had an amazing knowledge of local History. For example, she knew exactly where Lord Nelson's house had stood, with an underground passage linking it to Lady Hamilton's home. She also regaled me with all the gossip of their relationship, (whether I wished to hear it or not) - in such detail you'd think she had shared the house with them.

However, at eighty-three the old lady still had a mind and will of her own:

- "No, I am NOT having meals-on-wheels, don't know what they put in the stuff! Can't trust no one these days. John can just carry on cooking for me."

And her devoted son would bring in her shopping every evening after a hard day's work on a building site. She supervised and criticised while he cooked:

- "John, those are the wrong sausages AGAIN! Why didn't you go to my usual butcher's?... Much cheaper there." (As though the poor chap had nothing better to do!)

- "Because, Mum, he closed down five years ago, remember?"

70

John just carried on preparing her meal, taking no notice of her outbursts for he knew that his mother was lonely and in pain.

Encouraging the old lady to sing her favourite tunes was a great way of cheering her up. So while Flo was in the middle of an energetic albeit raucous rendition of "Daisy, Daisy, give me your answer, do. I'm 'alf crazy over the love of you!"... I would gently let myself out through the front door.

As time went by my friend's health gradually deteriorated. She was admitted into hospital and within a short while, passed away. I missed her company on Tuesdays, her stories of Merton in days gone by, her scolding and laughter.

Two years later, on the 23rd of December, I woke up in the morning earlier than usual. Still half asleep I wondered what time it was... only 6.30 a.m. on the alarm clock. But what had woken me up? Someone had nudged me... maybe it was a dream. Let's just turn over and go back to sleep.

But then, all of a sudden I sat up bold straight, wide awake this time, blinking in disbelief... for there, at the foot of my bed, in a luminous pink cloud, stood Flo, her eyes twinkling with laughter as she saw the astonishment on my face. This time my friend looked totally rejuvenated: her wrinkles had gone and her hair, although still white, was now thick and fluffy. Her skin had a healthy, rosy complexion. She was wearing a flowery blue cotton dress, with short sleeves and a white collar - fashionable in the forties.

The same shrewd blue eyes were observing me. Flo was chuckling with delight:

 - "Look, dearie... Here, I've come back to show you something!"

As I watched, mesmerised, she flung her left foot high up in the air then did the same with the other leg and finally pirouetted around like a ballerina. Then she added:

- "Now I want you to tell my son John that you saw me and that I am well. I am often in his house - still keeping an eye on him - so he'd better watch it! But reassure him that his recent problems will all clear within six months... and while you're at it wish him a Happy Christmas too."

Smiling I answered:

- "Okay, I'll pass on the message. It IS lovely to see you, Flo!"

Then she was gone. The pink cloud slowly disintegrated, fading away in the darkness. Nothing seemed to have changed in the bedroom.

Well, I wondered how on earth I could contact John Smith. There must be hundreds of them in the telephone directory and I did not even know where he lived. Dismayed, I thought: "John, where are you?" And, to top it all, before his mother's death he had told me that he was thinking of moving. But where to? England is a large place to go searching for a John Smith.

The best idea would be to meditate and ask Spirit for help. A quarter of an hour later I picked up the Telephone Directory and found the endless columns of "Smith"s. After three abortive calls I picked another number at random. This person lived locally.

- "Hello!" a man's voice answered.

- "Er... I am looking for a Mr John Smith, whose mother Florence was a neighbour of mine..."

- "Why, would you be speaking of my mother who passed away two years ago? I am Sidney, her other son. There were two of us, you know. My brother has moved away... No, you would never find his number because he is Ex-Directory. Well, here it is. Do you have a piece of paper?... And, by the way, the Season's Greetings to you, my dear. I hear you visited my mother and that she was fond of you..."

Then I phoned John. What on earth was I going to say? My heart missed a beat as I dialled his number. A woman's voice answered:

- "Yeah?"

- "Could I speak to John, please?"

 - "And who may YOU be?" she answered suspiciously.

- "No, don't worry. I am not a girl friend of his..."

Feeling like an absolute idiot I carried on:

- "I have a message from his mother..." (On Christmas Eve of all times! I felt more like one of the Three Wise Men announcing: "Rejoice! Rejoice! We bring you Good Tidings."

After a silence, she replied: "She's been dead for the past two years...

'Hey, John! There's a woman 'ere says she has a message from beyond the grave for you...."

Finally John came to the phone.

- "Hi, it's Muriel. Remember me?"

Yes, of course he did! (Thank goodness for that!) And when I told him what had happened, he was delighted:

- "We often feel Mum's presence around the house"... (and, to his wife): "Don't we, dear?"

- "Well, having passed on the message I shall now ring off. And, before I forget: A Happy Christmas on your mother's behalf, John!"

Never heard from him since. However, twice I received a message through another medium, just before Christmas:

- "Did you know an old lady with straight white hair? She was crippled down her left side. I get the name "Flo... no, Florence. She is wishing you a Happy Christmas!"

Let's hope Flo has found happiness in the Spirit World. I shall always remember her with affection for inside that tough old bird, there was plenty of love and laughter.

Clairvoyance

I shall now explain clairvoyance in more depth. As mentioned in the Introduction "Clair" means "clear" and "voyance" is "seeing" - so it's "clear seeing" people, objects and events that are not visible physically. A clairvoyant can feel past or future events but does not necessarily perceive deceased people whereas a medium has been especially trained to do so.

Not all mediums see these entities standing in front of them either. Most get an impression in their minds or hear messages telepathically. Really it's a matter of translating feelings into words.

For example, you think of a friend and all of a sudden the telephone rings and it's her. You have simply picked each other's thoughts.

A medium is a channel that relays messages. These do not derive from his/her own mind, nor from the sitter's. Communication may also come from - or for - a third party. For instance, an unknown Uncle Joe wants to let Mrs Jones down the road know that he did not commit suicide - it had been an accident - but that he is fine now. At this point the sitter has never heard of this person and must go and check with Mrs Jones - which can be somewhat embarrassing if he hardly knows her. The good lady in turn might be astonished, exclaiming: "Now wait until I tell my Auntie Maggie, his wife! She will be so relieved as she always knew he would never have taken his own life".

Joe was so desperate to get through to his partner that when he found the only channel available he simply barged in. I have often given similar messages that did not mean a thing to my clients but were of great joy to someone else. So, to say that I pick these messages from a sitter's brain is incorrect.

Clairvoyance requires a tremendous effort of concentration. It is often like sitting for an exam which can easily drain the medium. With some people the reading flows and with others it's very hard work. I always emphasise that my clairvoyance is only as good as the sitter is receptive. One should keep an open mind when consulting a medium.

Perhaps you desperately wish to hear from your mother and who comes through but cousin Bob whom you did not even get on with. A sensitive cannot order anyone to communicate from the other side unless they wish to do so. Maybe Mum was a shy introvert while Bob had always been a pushy character. In the Next World personalities do not change: Bob will still be elbowing his way through to the front of the queue. On the other hand, your mother may have only just passed recently after a long illness and is still resting, too weak to communicate. So in this case she may be grateful for cousin Bob's help.

All these factors should be taken into account. The average person is not going to sit at a graveside 24 hours a day. The same applies to spirits. They have to get on with their own busy life in the Next World and cannot always spare the time to communicate.

Some clients occasionally try to be as awkward as possible just to test me, in which case they make it hard not only for me but for themselves. One lady said: "I am going to be very lenient. As I close my eyes tell me exactly what I am thinking." (A good thing she did not know what I was thinking!) As politely as possible I answered:: "If I were that clever do you think I would be wasting my time giving you a reading? No, I'd be out there backing horses and making millions". She frowned: "Well, I warned you I would be difficult!" (You can say that again).

An unforgettable experience was provided by an elderly woman who came for a private sitting at the local church. She wore a flowery scarf on her head and an old fashioned blue coat. Clutching her holdall tightly on her lap, she sat down and leaned forward, her sharp eyes scrutinising me. My exact words were: "You worked in an ammunition factory during the war doing piece work... I have one of your colleagues here: his name is Albert and he is drinking a pint to your good health". The woman exclaimed: "Me? No, didn't work in no factory, dear. As to Albert: never heard of 'im. You could do a little better. Try again".

In those days I was still naive! Soon she had me almost in tears. Finally I shrugged and gave up: "Sorry, I have done my best. Obviously my standard of clairvoyance is not good enough. You'd better consult another medium". The old grannie got up and was just about to leave when, unexpectedly, she turned around at the door, laughing: "As a matter-of-fact, dearie, I did do piece work in a factory during the war and Albert worked there too. He had a soft spot for me, you know, and certainly liked his pint. Ha-Ha! Your reading wasn't bad." She winked: "Just testing to see how clever you are".

A medium proves survival after death and is not a fortuneteller. This gift requires intensive training and is a complex procedure involving the participation of higher beings from the Spirit World. So you can't just ask if you are going to win the Pools because the spirit helpers are not on that wavelength. They will give you a message relating to your spiritual progress and link you with your loved ones who have passed. It's not something you should dabble with even if you are psychic yourself. Either go for classes or leave well alone. If you don't control the gift, it will eventually control you.

Soon I realised that often, young people don't wish to hear from their ancestors: "Yes, that's my Gran alright. But she's had her life and I just want to know about mine".

Here is an extract from a young lady's letter: "Please let me know what is going to happen to me from this day onward for the rest of my life. Where am I going to live? How many lovers and husbands will I have? How many children - boys or girls? Will love last forever with a faithful husband; if not, how many mistresses will he have and will I find out? I also wish to know the date of my marriage and the colour of my husband's hair and eyes. Will he earn plenty of money or not? Tell me the lot: happiness, trouble, finances - except the deaths of my friends and family - that would scare me." (She'd certainly covered every eventuality!)

So I learned the Tarot cards as they enable me to give a more materialistic reading to those interested. When a young woman arrives in floods of tears because her boyfriend has left her, she wants upliftment and reassurance that life will improve and that she will meet someone else: for her, at that particular moment, it's the end of the world.

Of course, a pretty young thing will sooner or later find a new man to replace the previous one: this is not clairvoyance - anyone could tell her that - but when she sees for herself the "Lovers" card in her future she feels comforted. The cards are very accurate and I use them in conjunction with clairvoyance. The pictures should be interpreted symbolically. For example, the "Death" card represents the death of a situation: a new job, a move - it does not mean that someone is about to depart from this world. I never frighten anyone: my aim is to help and uplift. Often people ask: "If you see something terrible ahead will you tell me?" I would warn you in a roundabout way without frightening you if the problem can thus be avoided: "Drive more slowly and carefully. Concentrate on the road ahead and don't have your radio on".

Once I told a sitter that she would be burgled: "I see a man putting his hand through the kitchen window at the rear of your house. He is unlocking the door and letting himself in... Now please go home and add locks to both your kitchen window and door and you will be safe." She obviously dismissed my prediction for the following week, that same lady was on the phone: "Muriel, guess what. I was burgled today... just as you said. The chap put his hand through the kitchen window and let himself in... he stole the television set and the video in front of my father who was fast asleep in his fireside chair. He never woke up!" Now she has had new locks installed and a burglar alarm!

It is totally against my principles to tell someone: "You are going to die in six months' time" - even if the person has a terminal illness and probably won't last much longer. I always offer hope and encouragement. It has been my privilege on several occasions to hold a dying friend's hand and see her husband, her mother or other loved ones coming to fetch her. At that stage the patient can often see them too and the joy on both sides is wonderful.

Chapter Six

When I joined Bill's circle he advised us, as part of our training, to meditate every evening for ten minutes. He also told us to keep a list of sick people who requested absent healing. Every night before the meditation we were to read out each name in turn visualising the patient recovering. It all seemed rather far fetched but I dutifully did my homework. How could reading out a list of names make anyone feel better? I was quite sceptical, to say the least. Yet, to my own incredulity, after a short while I was ticking off names one by one as each patient's condition improved.

It was not easy to ignore the pile of ironing in the kitchen... the letters to write... and a dozen other matters that suddenly seemed so urgent. My mind would be distracted: now where had that layer of dust suddenly come from on top of the dresser when I had not noticed it earlier on? I'll just get a duster...it won't take a minute... No, LEAVE IT! (But I don't like dust!)

Jake, another student, was not so fortunate. When he tiptoed upstairs into the bedroom one of his four children would call out:

- "Dad! What are you doing up there?"

- "I am meditating!"

- "What's that?"

- "Being still".

- "What for?"

- "Because I have to".

- "But my bike has broken down. Can't you come and fix it?"

- "Later".

- "But I need it NOW!"

And his daughter would join in: "Dad, can I come upstairs and talk to you? Will you read me a book?"

- "As soon as I've finished MEDITATING!"

- "Mum!... Why won't Dad read me a book? I think I am going to cry".

Finally, his wife would call up the stairs: "Jake. Dinner's ready! Why on earth does Bill make you waste time like that..."

In the end Jake had to give up his classes to maintain the peace at home.

My first introduction to meditation had come in my early twenties when I spent a few week-ends with an Indian family. At 4 a.m., one of the guests, Mr Chandra, a wizened man with a splendid moustache, would rise and perform noisy ablutions in the bathroom, after which he'd sit cross-legged in the Lotus position on his bed, leaving his bedroom door open. This was followed by a session on his head with his feet up against the wall. (And, yes, in case you're interested, he kept his dhoti - or loincloth - well tied up). His face would turn a bright crimson anyway.

I would have carried on sleeping blissfully but for Mr Chandra's unfortunate custom of also playing a plaintive tune on a reed pipe. This may have been a splendid way of greeting a new dawn on the Ganges but the effect was somehow dampened down in London suburbia on a cold, wet, Winter morning.

Soon the baby would wake up screaming while the whole household, grumbling and cursing, told their guest to belt up. The whole set-up was colourful and entertaining. Afterwards I'd keep nodding off to sleep at work.

It was only years later that I started to take meditation seriously - the purpose of the exercise being more than just staring at one's navel in an uncomfortable position. In fact, it's the basis of all spiritual work. Until then my life had been in two dimensions: meditation opened the door to a third one. You can't just sit down for ten minutes and expect great things to happen - they won't. It's a question of being still regularly over a period of time. This slowly builds up energy in the room just as a car needs petrol. You can look at a vehicle as much as you like but without fuel it won't start. Visions and materialisations seem to work on the same principle, only it's the sitter who provides the fuel from his own energy. Historical saints had visions because they spent long hours praying in isolation. So you obviously have to be very sensitive yourself to start off with.

Meditation is like lighting an innocuous wick that leads all the way to a powder keg and... BANG! an explosion powerful enough to blow up any Bridge on the River Kwai ensues. All of a sudden stories of angels and Biblical heroes come to life: they materialise out of the blue. The whole thing was astounding. As barriers of time disappeared I could hardly believe my eyes. Only my practical Taurean approach told me it was not a dream. I expected actors like Richard Burton in Roman costume to walk in to the sound of Aida's Triumphant March... a Cecil B. De Mille production in all its splendour... but no, this was no Hollywood story. What I saw was genuine, simple and often silent, which made it all the more baffling.

So through deep breathing and stilling of the mind in a peaceful atmosphere, energy - or ectoplasm - builds up charging the room over a period of time with something similar to electricity. Its presence can be felt and almost touched - an awe inspiring experience. You find yourself whispering as you would inside a cathedral. The power increases steadily until all of a sudden the door is flung wide open into another dimension. A parallel can be drawn with the story of Alice in Wonderland who stepped through the looking glass into another world.

There are various ways of meditating with strict rules and regulations. (I won't bore you with the details.) Join a reputable meditation group. Basically if you are seeking inner peace then concentrate on a white light which you imagine on top of your head. If you are interested in clairvoyance bring the light down between your eyes.

Don't experiment on your own because you are linking in with another dimension which must be kept under control. Some sitters will meditate for years and see nothing at all - depending on their degree of sensitivity. It's rather like tuning into a distant radio station. With some receivers you will be lucky and with others you won't.

The following events are all authentic - as incredible and far fetched as they may seem. If anyone had told me similar stories I too would have laughed them off: "Ha-ha! Tell us another". After all when Marco Polo came back from China with his strange tales everyone thought he was mad. All I can say is that I am telling the truth and that is all that matters.

Practice was difficult at first. Every evening I'd sit down alone in my lounge wondering how to control my restless mind. But with perseverance and soft music I would drift off and come back an hour later... a new and exhilarating experience... definitely not sleep as I was often still conscious of my surroundings. Over a period of weeks a wonderfully peaceful atmosphere permeated the room. Even today it's the first thing visitors remark upon. There was companionship in the silence and I never felt alone. Benign presences were watching over me.

After a while bright patches of colour started to flicker across the room. A few weeks later, as soon as my eyes were closed I could distinctly see people, as though a television set had been switched on in my mind. They would come close in turn for a few seconds until I could distinguish their face in detail before floating away to make room for the next person. At least a dozen human beings of all nationalities would show themselves in this way. They seemed pensive, not at all frightening. Upon opening my eyes I could still see their image reflected in the room.

Bill explained: "The healing thoughts you send off every night form a shaft of light on the Astral which lost spirits can see. Some of them have been wandering around for ages. They are attracted to the glow like moths to a lamp. Just pray for them, imagining a pathway of light going towards the sun and redirect them on that road. It will guide them safely to the Next World."

Simple enough. The power was building up in my front room. I could feel it... Oh, dear. Whatever next? On one occasion as soon as I shut my eyes I saw a whole boatload of Vietnamese refugees. It was pitiful: they looked totally lost and weary. One sad face after another came close in turn while I sent them off to the light: elderly couples clinging to each other, mothers with babies, children sucking their thumb as they stared at me in shock. Even with my eyes open I could still see the shadow of a large fishing boat upon the wall. These people were aware of me as I was of them, a strangely moving experience. It seemed like ages until the last one, a withered old man, had been dispatched.

And then they were all gone and the picture of the vessel slowly faded away. I wondered how many more had drowned and were still lost in space.

A week later I had another strange encounter in the gathering dusk. The room was quiet and peaceful. I was just having a mug of coffee and reading a book when I looked up and noticed with surprise a pale, skinny man standing behind the television set gazing at me. He was not physical i.e. he looked rather like the proverbial transparent ghost in stories.

My guest had a long white beard; he was stark naked and emaciated, his ribcages sticking out. As he drew closer I realised with a shock that he was still a young man in his late twenties. Greeting him I enquired: "God bless you, friend, what can I do for you?" (This simple phrase neutralises whatever power you are facing). His reply came swiftly: "Help, I am lost!"

Soon half a dozen other people appeared out of nowhere: pale, bewildered men and women - they were little more than skeletons. One person was wearing striped pyjamas. Then I understood: they were Jewish prisoners from a nazi concentration camp still wandering around in time. These sad ghosts surrounded me, coming so close that they overshadowed me. For a split second our souls touched and blended - their despair became mine. Gently I coaxed them: "Can you see a faint glow ahead? Then go towards it. You are free now. No one can harm you anymore"... Still in a daze they obediently floated towards the light in file where their shape slowly dissolved within its glow. They had finally reached the end of their traumatic journey and found peace... a very moving experience as I watched them disappear. Since then other Jewish prisoners have followed and were redirected too.

I developed my own method of sending out absent healing every night, imagining the patient smiling as he gets out of bed to stand underneath a shower of blue light. He looks up happily while the beneficial rays envelop him. This is visualised prayer and very effective. Mumbling a few holy verses does not mean much unless you are sincere and send out love at the same time. Within a few minutes of concentration the patient can usually feel a pleasant warm energy - even if he lives miles away - and he starts to recover.

On several occasions I have been on the receiving end of healing. Once I was in hospital in intensive care after a road accident. All of a sudden a warm electrical current came flowing up my arms and legs. It returned half an hour later as someone else was thinking of me. Already I was starting to feel more lively. A while later more healing came and I sat up in bed, the temperature gone.

The nurse's mouth dropped open when, smiling, I asked for a cup of tea. She ran off and came back shortly afterwards with the doctor. He examined me, perplexed: "Well, I never"... was all he muttered under his breath. He in turn called his colleague for a second opinion. Both men and the nurse stood around my bed shaking their heads in astonishment. Two days later I was discharged.

Healing is universal: it is simply the power of love and works both with and without religious beliefs.

Relaxing on my own that hot July evening I drifted into meditation. An hour or so later I opened my eyes. On the table a large bunch of carnations received from a friend brightened up the room in the subdued light. The atmosphere was quiet and pleasantly peaceful. As I looked at the flowers absent-mindedly they seemed to move slightly... but how could they? There was no draught... Sitting up straight I peered intently at the shadows. The outline of a man was now gradually building up in front of the table. I could see him clearly although he had no physical substance. (Imagine an actor stepping out of a film and standing in front of you like a hologram. The image is not flat, the person is there. You can communicate but if you went close enough you'd walk straight through him. That is the best description I am able to give).

My visitor had grey, matted, shoulder length hair. He wore breeches and a frayed white shirt with long sleeves and an open neckline. He could have done with a bath and a visit to the launderette. Here was a middle aged man in a state of great agitation for he kept gesticulating and muttering to himself as he paced up and down. Definitely Continental!

Suddenly, to my surprise, he turned around and fell to his knees in front of me: "Mille fois pardon, Madame, je vous implore. Venez a mon secours". In his quaint flowery French he begged me to help him: "I have been wandering around in total darkness for many moons. You are the first person I see and my only hope of salvation"...

Yes, he was truly from a bygone era. (Now in this scene D'Artagnan would have bowed, sweeping off his feathered hat with great panache... Keep cool, Muriel. Don't start giggling... it's not funny - well, how would YOU have coped in the circumstance, alone face to face with a French ghost from another century?)

Fascinated I answered: - "Bonsoir, Monsieur. God bless you. Please tell me your name".

- "I am Jodin, J-O-D-I-N". He spelled each letter separately to make sure I'd understood.

- "Well, Mr Jodin. I shall do my best to help you by visualising a pathway of light. If you see even a faint glimmer go towards it and you will be safe.

The minute I started to concentrate... hey, presto! he vanished. Now where had he gone to? That's all I needed.

Dismayed, I called out:

- "Mr Jodin! Where are you?"

He returned almost immediately and once more went down on his knees. This time he was beaming with delight: - "I have seen the light! Pray accept my eternal gratitude, chere Madame" - and with that he disappeared.

What a night! Not many people have all these ghostly adventures in their front room before going to bed.

Not to be outdone, I went straight to the Reference Library the following morning to discover who this mysterious visitor may well be. And, sure enough... found him! There was his name in the encyclopedia, a Frenchman indeed: our Monsieur Jodin was a general in Napoleon's army. He fought in most of the Emperor's campaigns then, for some obscure reason, fell in disgrace and committed suicide. It all fitted into place! The poor chap had been wandering in space all this time. Indeed, he had met his Waterloo!

These are only a few rescue stories. There have been so many I could write ghost stories on a conveyor belt. Ever wished you too could see a spirit? There is a very easy way. Just turn off the main light in your sitting room and leave a side-lamp on. In the silence, look at your television set when it is switched off. You will see the reflection of the room on its screen... there may also be a shadow somewhere in the picture. It looks like a person... Turn around and check the room. No, at that spot there is only a flower pot on top of a cupboard.

Now return to the screen... yes, the shadow is definitely building up... a man in period costume clearly visible. He is poring over a book, flicking the pages. At this point your guests will be able to see this ghost too, whether they are psychic or not. It's probably something to do with the electricity around the set. I can't guarantee you will see a ghost on a regular basis, but keep on trying. You should be successful within a short while.

Another interesting experiment obtained through meditation is Astral Travelling. While my body was relaxing on the settee my soul was miles away. It felt wonderful travelling, swooped up into space as on a magic carpet. Slowly, a blurred picture would come into focus and I would land in the middle of the scenery. Once I found myself standing alone on a mountainside watching a rainbow across the valley. Its soft hues were etched over a waterfall cascading down the rocks. At a guess I was somewhere in South America judging by the heat, the steam and the dense tropical vegetation glistening in the rain.

On another occasion I was floating through hospital wards stopping at every bed. Perhaps the patients had a terminal illness - they all looked pale and sick. Silently I sent healing to each of them in turn while they remained unaware of my presence. Anyway none of them pulled the sheets over their head screaming: "Nurse, help! I've seen a ghost... right over THERE!".

When it was time to wake up in the morning I felt shattered. Once I landed high up in the Himalayas where a group of Tibetan monks were sitting in a circle, meditating in the morning mist. One of them, an enigmatic Lama with a pointed hat and a grey beard, was turning a prayer wheel. The air was frosty and I shivered. They moved over to make room for me and I sat crosslegged between them. Unlike the patients in the hospital, these gentlemen were aware of me and could actually see me too! How extraordinary! I still don't know whether I was seeing a picture in time or whether these monks are alive and well in Tibet today. If you have the answer please let me know.

And so I have travelled all over the world in between the housework. It certainly saves on air fares. No one knows what goes on behind closed doors! At a glance I must have looked just like any other single mother struggling to bring up her children on her own.

Why do men automatically think that a divorced woman is ready to jump into bed with them? A wiry, bald headed Sicilian called Emilio knew exactly what HE wanted. Obviously thinking I was desperate he moaned in the street:

- "My wife, she doesn't understand me. In fact we've just had another row". (I wondered if they had any plates left!)
"Tell you what. I do shift work and have decided to come and visit you every afternoon from two to six. I earn lots of money and am prepared to pay for what you offer me".

Just like that! Did he expect me to be flattered at the offer of sharing his siesta or should I bash him on the head with my handbag? In the end, diplomacy prevailed: "No, sorry, you have a very nice wife and I am not interested. Try and make it up with her".

- "Think it over", he insisted, "it would help with the bills".

What cheek! The following day his wife saw me in the supermarket. She seemed quite forlorn and under the weather.

- "How are you, Rosa? Pop in for coffee sometime". (Was I trying to be sympathetic, show her I was on her side and that she had nothing to fear?)

- "Muriel, I would-da love that" she replied.

84

The following Wednesday morning the bell rang and there was Rosa looking as fed up as ever, in her sensible lace-up shoes and shabby black coat.

I invited her in. Over coffee and biscuits she commented:

- "Povre! It-ta must-ta be very lonely here on your own with your two bambinos". (Can't do the Italian accent!) "What a pity your marriage did not work out".

- "Oh, I don't know. Can't complain, really. Anyhow, lots of married people are lonely too".

- "Not-ta when you have found THE right man, as I have with my Emilio!".

Why, she was boasting of the same man who had propositioned me a few days earlier!

(No, of course not: I never breathed a word!)

Chapter Seven

Return to Ancient Egypt

My attitude towards ghosts is: Keep cool. Don't panic or be afraid. They can't harm you anyway. Be kind and helpful but firm as it is usually you who are doing them a favour. Spirits are often more afraid of you than you are of them.

One of my latest nocturnal callers left me puzzled. Why had he come? My powers to help him were so limited. One minute I was alone, relaxing with a cup of tea, and the next a nebulous form was taking shape in front of me. Putting down the cup I sat up and called gently:

- "God bless you friend, what can I do for you? Please come forward". (By now I was feeling the confidence of an Old Timer!)

It took a while before the blue misty shape managed to take on a human form. He must have come from a long way off in the Next Realms so had difficulty in reaching the dense atmosphere of the earth. This spirit was wrapped up in a pale blue cloth and looked like a skeleton covered with a shrivelled up skin. He had long eyelashes and now proceeded to scrutinise me with piercing, intelligent eyes that were very much alive, if a little sad.

My guest must have understood my invitation for he slowly came closer until we were virtually nose to nose. Not at all put off by his proximity, I reached out and touched his face as this is what he wished me to do. It felt surprisingly sticky.

- "Are you a mummy? How interesting! I have seen some like you in the British Museum", I said cheerfully.

He conveyed to me that my guess was correct. His message came telepathically. He said that the souls of Ancient Egyptians were still hovering around their mummies, resenting the flow of tourists staring irreverently at their remainders. They now wish to be buried again and prayers offered for their peace.

Having delivered his case the ghost then slowly faded away in front of my eyes. His instructions left me perplexed. What on earth could I do to help? Simply phone the curator of the British Museum and announce casually: "I have a

My bubbly Welsh friend Gwyneria. She had developed the gift of automatic writing and drawing. I watched, fascinated, as she drew strange maps of Ancient Egypt, though she did not know this at the time. Subsequently I was to be transported back to the 1st Dynasty.

message from the mummies in your Egyptian Department. They object to their present treatment and wish to be buried in style". (Just imagine his face... and his comments: "We have another nutcase here".)

There was only one single option open: the D.I.Y. one. So this is how I wound my way to the British Museum where I said a prayer in front of every single mummy and, visualising blue healing light encircling each of them in turn I asked for a blessing and peace to be restored.

It wasn't much but if anyone has a better idea they are welcome to contact the curator.

At the time Gwyneira, a bubbly Welsh friend of mine, came to visit me regularly. We had known each other for several years and I loved her dynamism, her Rhumley Valley accent and her Indian Khaftans. She was a tonic on a grey day, making me giggle with her funny stories. We have remained firm friends ever since.

Surprise, surprise! Gwyneira had also discovered clairvoyance at the same time and was now attending development classes. To me, a mere novice, she was a great authority on the subject so I carefully followed all her instructions.

After a leisurely meal and a chat over a cup of tea we would meditate in the front room. My friend would bring me the odd watch or ring to psychometrize. Holding the article and giving off whatever meagre inspiration came to my mind was an effort of concentration. However, Gwyneira would encourage me enthusiastically.

She had acquired the skill of automatic writing and drawing. Fascinated, I watched as she drew strange shapes. What could they be? Never seen anything like it before! After a while names were added to the drawings and we realised that my friend had been sketching maps of ancient Egypt. Explanations from Spirit were soon to follow as she started to write page after page at an increasing pace - her hand was shaking with the power and seemed to have been put on "Pilot" - no one could have written this fast. Perspiring with the effort she had no idea what was going to come through next.

If Gwyneira can do automatic writing, so can I! (Or so I decided). Try as I would all I ever wrote was a series of squiggles spelling out "m-e-n-e-s" over and over again and nothing else. Disappointed, I gave up. (That should teach you, Muriel!) It was only a few months later that quite by chance I happened to glance through a book on Egyptian History. A few words caught my attention:

"King Menes, lst Dynasty, 3200 BC". What a revelation! It certainly boosted my morale.

After my usual evening meditation I yawned, stretched and glancing at the clock. decided it was time to go to bed. But, hold on, what was that strange mist over there in the corner near the dresser? Instant fog of the type sprayed at Rock concerts was bellowing out in front of the furniture. (Was I going mad?) It quickly spread out in front of the furniture from floor to ceiling like a large vapourous grey screen. At the same time the room grew very cold and I shivered... My heart was racing and I felt myself being drained of energy. Whatever was happening it was drawing on my own strength. My eyes were rivetted to this ghostly screen, drawing me like a magnet.

Then, to my astonishment a faded, three-dimensional film in slow motion appeared. As the view became clearer so did I feel weaker. Now a wide suspended terrace with a large semicircular series of steps leading to the edge of a cliff was gradually becoming visible. Where the steps joined flowers and small trees had been carefully planted. In the background green shrubs and palm trees stood outlined against the blue sky. Two men were in that scenery: one carrying an urn on his shoulder while the other was bending over weeding a patch of plants. According to their clothing they must have been Egyptian slaves.

The penny dropped: this was actually a picture in time straight out of Ancient Egypt! And it was drawing me irresistibly just as if I were a vegetable peeling spiralling with the dishwater down a giant kitchen plughole. What would happen if I simply gave in and allowed myself to enter the picture? Would I die to this life and go back in time? However, my curiosity had its limits... for if I did not react quickly I would lose control altogether and pass out. So I made a terrific effort and managed to get up.

- "God bless you, now please go away!" I commanded rather unconvincingly. Slowly, the picture gradually disintegrated and disappeared altogether.

It took a while before the room felt warm again and I regained my strength. My reflection in the mirror showed someone pale enough to frighten a ghost!

When Gwyneira paid me a visit the following Saturday she was bubbling over with a new idea. Curled up on the settee with a mug of tea in one hand and a cigarette in the other she told me her plan: "The other day I was shown how to do Psychometry with a plant. Could you go and cut a small branch from the cherry-tree outside and rub it in your hands? I will do the same and then we shall exchange the twigs and see what happens".

90

Great! We both went into the garden, came back, sat down and exchanged our trophies. I held Gwyneira's branch... Mmm... it seemed to emit a powerful energy. This was certainly more alive than a piece of jewellery. Almost immediately I was once more facing the suspended gardens of Ancient Egypt. A pair of black curtains trimmed with gold were hanging at a short distance from each other from the top of the cliff all the way down to the ground below. (I thought: "How ridiculous! These curtains should be blowing away in the wind.")

A woman was slowly gliding into sight... her features seemed somehow familiar... yes, she was Gwyneira's double, distinctly recognisable! She stood still, surveying her surroundings - an elegant apparition in a long black dress. Her dark hair was pulled back in a bun adorned with two bright peacock feathers. Elaborate ear-rings and a matching necklace enhanced her beauty. Behind her stood a dwarf holding up a parasol. Here was this down-to-earth Welsh friend of mine perfectly recognisable but with the airs and graces of a queen! Amazed, I described the scenery to the 20th century Gwyneira sitting beside me.

Earlier on, her automatic writing had revealed that in a previous incarnation she had been Queen Minny, wife of the king who had united the Upper and Lower Kingdoms of Egypt (whoever he may be). Being the more inquisitive of the two I looked up the information in the Public Library and discovered that the Pharaoh responsible for this achievement was... none other than King Menes. Minny may have been a distortion of Menes - or perhaps its female version.

I contacted the Egyptian Department of the British Museum. A helpful man at the end of the telephone looked up all the information available on King Menes. He said that, as far as he knows, there is no written record of the name of this Pharaoh's wife. It all happened so long ago... all of 5,200 years ago.

Back at home and another session of meditation with Gwyneira: this time I was transported to the foot of the cliff where the queen, still elegant in black, was now going down the steps at the foot of the curtains and disappeared into a dark chamber. She seemed preoccupied - at a guess she was checking the arrangements for her husband's funeral.

Hammering was going on somewhere in the background as craftsmen were putting the finishing touches to their work... I could feel signs of feverish activity although no one was to be seen. Like a shadow I followed Queen Minny down a long corridor. We seemed to carry on for ages. At first I could see nothing but after a while my eyes grew accustomed to the darkness. In the shadows I suddenly came face to face with a large statue of Anubis, the Jackal god with pointed ears, guardian of the threshold to the Underworld. His eyes were alert; he looked straight at me as though to ask: "What are YOU doing here?" (And not: "Do you come here often?" - or: "What is a gorgeous chick like you doing in a place like this?"- or else: "Do you have a light, mate?" - suddenly I was thinking up the most ridiculous comments to steady my nerves).

The walls were freshly painted with frescoes. The smell of varnish, wood and incense was overpowering. Two other formidable statues of gods loomed further ahead... At this stage I was starting to feel increasingly tired, drained and faint as once more the vision took up all my energy. So, reluctantly I decided to adjourn the session and return to 20th century London. The climax of this tale occurred a fortnight later when I sat meditating on my own. Suddenly I was projected back in time again. On this occasion I had a glimpse of a royal barge in the mist silently floating across a river. Presumably it was transporting the Pharaoh's sarcophagus - although I could not get close enough to check. The scenery changed and I found myself in the middle of a cortege of Egyptians, ceremoniously bearing the King's coffin towards the foot of the same cliff.

The black curtains were still in place. Again I was following Gwyneira now being carried in style on a litter. (She reminded me of Elizabeth Taylor in "Cleopatra"). As we approached the end of the journey, bald headed priests dressed in white greeted us to the sound of raucous trumpets. We were reaching the end of our destination. Ahead, Queen Minny was disappearing into the tomb followed by her court. When it came to my turn in the queue I suddenly rebelled. What lay ahead? Yes, it all came back now... there would be poison to drink so that we could accompany the Pharaoh into the Next World.

Was it despair that made me panic and scream out aloud: "NO! This time I REFUSE to enter..." Shaking with fear, I watched the cortege coming to an abrupt halt as priests, musicians and other dignitaries turned around slowly and stared at me in utter amazement and disbelief.

The shock had catapulted me out of Egypt and back into this era. Gratefully, I opened my eyes, relieved to see my familiar surroundings. For once the sound of a car outside was music to my ears.

I telephoned Gwyneira and she was fascinated: "Did you also know that I had a son called Musjot? And that he is the entity who now guides my hand to draw? And... yes, your information tallies with mine: only a few days ago the automatic writing revealed that I had been entombed alive.

92

Many years later a medium told me in a reading: "By the way, do you know you were once a High Priestess in Ancient Egypt? Those were happy days when you sang and danced in the Temple. Having the gift of prophecy you were wise and respected: people came from miles away for guidance. This is why you love to sing aloud today." (True! But how did he know? He had never met me before in his life.) "Ever thought of becoming a medium? It would only be a matter of picking up the threads where you left off in a previous life"... As an afterthought he added: "You lived in the lst Dynasty"...

The Dynasty of King Menes! It all fitted into place.

P.S. - "Tell us another", you may scoff after reading this chapter. So would I if it hadn't happened to me! However, the story is true, whatever you may think to the contrary. I have described the events as accurately as possible. Take it or leave it: I don't mind.

l. If I had imagined it all I would have stuck to historically safe details: Gwyneira would be wearing a traditional black wig instead of a bun adorned with peacock feathers. After all I really don't know if that hairstyle was in vogue at the time, but that is how she was. Her long black dress was probably a toga or a simple piece of material gathered at the waist.

2. Maybe I saw the Valley of Kings but it could have been somewhere else. There was no road sign anywhere! However, whereas today the area is a desert, in my vision palm trees grew and a garden with half circular steps led down to the top of the cliffs.

3. A pair of black curtains trimmed with gold hung motionless from the top of the cliffs right down to either side of the entrance to the tomb. "That's impossible!", I thought. "Even if the drapes are secured why aren't they blowing in the wind?" Then I remembered the words of an old Desert Rat friend:

 - "It was stifling hot and still. Nothing moved. There was not even the merest puff of wind"...

4. Recently I read the story of a woman who went to Egypt where she encountered the spirit of a Pharaoh... dressed in a BLUE CLOTH - the symbol of Royalty.

... So who was the ghostly mummy who paid me a visit? He arrived shortly before these visions took place as though to introduce them. There is no doubt that they are interlinked in this tale - so powerful that it left its imprint in time.

Could he have been King Menes? He never gave me his name. I leave it for you to decide.

At first only great pharaohs and holy people were mummified and revered in the belief that they would bring good fortune to their followers. (Even today many people have faith in the miraculous properties of saints' relics - in fact the Vatican has a Library of holy remainders, all neatly filed away.)

Later on mummification became the height of fashion so that everyone who was someone wishing to keep up with the Egyptian Joneses made arrangements to be mummified after their demise. Even household pets were honoured with the same treatment. The Egyptians were convinced that they would only be reincarnated in Amenti - or Heaven - if their whole body was preserved so it was carefully marinated in herbs, spices and resin and finally wrapped up in bandages while the viscera were kept in a separate jar.

The same principle applied to paintings: the shape of the whole body had to be visible in the picture if the subject were to attain eternity - which is why an Egyptian would be seen walking in profile with his stomach twisted around to face the artist.

Embalming was a lengthy and expensive process so the Egyptians made sure that their property was adequately protected against robbers and future archaeologists alike. Anyone found plundering a grave was swiftly dispatched to the Next World. Some tombs were dug so deep in the ground that they still have not been discovered today.

How was this protection achieved? Physically: by building solid constructions, lengthy corridors, false walls, trapdoors etc. and psychically: with the help of thought forms and the invocation of Elements.

When the first archaeologists entered a tomb, at their great moment of personal glory, they also disturbed the protective energy surrounding the entrance.

In the British Museum I remember seeing a large upright stone slab in a corner. Even from a distance I was aware of a dark pulsating shadow surrounding it, making me shudder. I still took a closer look and eventually touched it... the stone felt alive but somehow I knew it would not harm me because I was treating it with respect. An explanatory note was stuck on the wall: the slab was believed to be the entrance to a tomb.

So, collectors of ethnic artifacts should be cautious for a beautiful wooden mask brought back from darkest Africa or a pot from a South American tomb could be cursed and the souvenir hunter may have brought back more than he bargained for.

———————

A while ago I went on a guided tour of the Egyptian section of the British Museum. This event was organised by Jim Bennett, an archaeologist. It was a wonderful opportunity for me to ask questions of this knowledgeable man. Not only did he give us an interesting talk but, much to my delight, he could also read and translate hieroglyphics.

Towards the end of the visit I asked our guide: "There is a stone slab in a corner I would like you to see. Could you possibly spare the time and come and have a look at it?"

- "Why, certainly" he replied amiably.

So I dragged him along to the slab mentioned earlier: "I don't know why, but this stone makes me shudder. It gives me a cold, uneasy feeling."

Jim was poring over the piece of rock: "Hmmm...that's interesting. Look at the Egyptian couple engraved here... and, yes! They have been deliberately defaced. So it is obvious that these two must have done something drastically wrong to be so unpopular. This is amazing, I must say... an instance where the Psychic and the Scientific meet." (Perhaps people believed at the time that by defacing the two statues the couple would be prevented from entering the Hereafter.)

As he was such a pleasant man I ventured to ask him if he would read this chapter of my book and criticise it - to which he readily agreed.

When Jim returned the papers his comments were: "I can't find anything inaccurate except one detail that puzzles me: the semi-circular steps - as all Egyptian constructions were square - never circular. On the other hand a suspended terrace of that shape would fit in well with Mesopotamia... so maybe the first Egyptians came from that country. This is really interesting because it may fill a historical gap as we are not sure where the first Egyptians originated from."

My children were growing up. Life was more settled. As any mother knows housework takes up a lot of time. Ah! For the services of a maid, a cook, a nurse and a butler instead of being all of these rolled into one! Still, I would not have missed any of it as I shared my boys' joys and upsets and all their achievements. Can't see the point in the British Empire upbringing: a nanny to look after them up to the age of 7 when they are packed off to boarding school. Mum then gives all her affection to her dogs. With all due respect to the pets, the kids also need love and care.

My boys represented a lot of work and sacrifices when they were younger but we had some great times together and now that they are both grown up they are super company.

A mother can never see her child as grown-up. One of my treasured memories is watching my father, then middle aged and bald, waltzing in the hall to the sound of the Blue Danube, with Gran, then nearly 80. The delight on her face was wonderful to see.

Here is a poem I wrote at the time:

Nathan

Three long, three short - six times the bell rang.
At the door I heard a Crash! and a Bang!

A little grubby face, a broad smile,
Rosy cheeks, shiny eyes: "I've run a mile

To come home to you, Mum, I'm so hot".
He flung down his satchel: "Look what I've got:

Here's Treasure Island, drawn just for you
With a bunch of flowers, yellow and blue".

I looked at the map, the weeds so fair,
The torn trousers and dishevelled hair...

Then hugged that little angel, gave him a kiss:
He was my Treasure, in that second of bliss.

Nathan has inherited my father's temperament. It's quite touching watching him react just like Dad, reading the same books and taking an interest in similar subjects.

My father passed away shortly after I wrote this poem.

Dad's Farewell

Suddenly my father died of a heart attack and my world crumbled apart. Somehow I thought dear old Dad was invincible and would last forever like the Pyramids or the great Wall of China. He'd always been there at the end of the phone to listen to my problems and come up with the answers.

Mother only notified his friends after the funeral simply because she could not face hundreds of mourners turning up and besides her husband was a simple man who would have hated all the fuss.

So back I was in Ghent with my eternal suitcase. Word had gone around the neighbourhood like wildfire and when the cortege drove slowly away crowds appeared from nowhere and silently lined the pavement to pay their last respects to Frank - a good friend who'd helped them all at sometime.

A strange thing happened the evening before the funeral. A room had been set aside for the coffin, the wall covered with Royal Blue velvet. As I stood there with my mother she asked:

- "Would you like to lift the lid and take a last look at Dad?"

- "No thank you", I answered firmly.

Mum shrugged her shoulders, disappointed and left the room. The sound of her footsteps echoed as she went back upstairs to her flat.

Left alone I sat down next to the coffin feeling quite lost. After a while the silence intensified. Slowly I grew aware of invisible people chatting excitedly all around me in a party atmosphere. Their joy was infectious. Then I realised that while we were sad to lose such a good man, others were delighted as they prepared for his arrival. It was then that I felt the presence of my grandmother who had come to fetch her son. She was fussing over him and so he would be well looked after. Already I was feeling much better, grateful for this wonderful gift of clairvoyance.

A few months after my father's death I returned to Belgium in July to visit my mother. How empty home would be without my dear Dad. As the jetfoil arrived in Ostend I remembered with sadness not to look out for him, waving happily from the pier. He would always have given me a big hug before chatting about his affairs, his customers and his friends:

- "The car is parked just outside. Now come on, tell me all the latest news."

This time I must remember to take the train in Ostend. We were entering the port and gliding alongside fishing boats. Seagulls circled around screeching in the sky. The jetfoil was packed with tourists who were commenting excitedly at the scenery. Yes, Ostend was certainly picturesque, I suppose, if one is in the right frame of mind.

All of a sudden the air around me felt very cold. Shivers ran down my spine although it was a warm summer day... (The doors had not been opened yet to produce such a draught - the passengers were still wearing their seat belts...)

And then I saw him, standing in front of me near the window: my dear old Dad, in his favourite old brown hat and raincoat, holding out his arms - the same face and wise eyes, yet somehow different: his wrinkles had gone, he was now slim with brown hair whereas he'd been bald in his latter years. He smiled with emotion: "Welcome home, Muriel. See: I'm still the first here to greet you. Be patient with your mother as she is getting on"... And then he vanished as suddenly as he had appeared.

The air around me felt warm again. Dad's presence had been so real for perhaps just one minute. Now it was back to the hustle and bustle on the boat. The doors opened, the passengers collected their hand luggage and proceeded down the ramp.

I was the only holiday-maker getting off the jetfoil with tears in my eyes.

Chapter Eight

One recognises budding mediums by their keenness to be of assistance to others. After a while this zest is somewhat tempered down by caution: - "Oh, yes? I see... hmm" (weighing the pros and the cons) instead of exclaiming: "Oh, no. You can't possibly be serious! Let me help."

How many times has a suicidal person phoned me in the throes of despair sobbing that unless I see her IMMEDIATELY she will swallow the contents of the bottle of pills in front of her. So I urgently cancel my next booking with apologies and then proceed to wait... and wait... and wait. No one turns up.

When I finally give up watching the clock and phone the desperate lady, she laughs uneasily:

- "My boyfriend has arrived and we have made it up. I feel better now"...

Or else: - "Sorry, can't stop and talk. I am just off to a pub with a friend".

- "Why didn't you phone to let me know? I've stayed in all afternoon and lost a booking because of you".

- "Oh... well, I didn't think".

Oh, yes, I was learning fast! So when a neighbour rang my doorbell in a state of panic, I remained calm:

- *"Muriel, quick! Maggie is going to kill herself. She says she is determined to jump out of the window. I can't reason with her. Perhaps you could try". (The poor woman was desperately tugging at my sleeve.)*

- *"Okay. I am coming. Just let me put my coat on". (It was the middle of winter).*

So off I trotted, following Kay in the snow.

- *"Where does she live?*

- *"On the third floor over there. Hurry up! We may be too late. (By now Kay was running).*

Maggie's front door was unlocked and we let ourselves in. In the dusk I could see a woman in her sixties who was reclining on a dilapidated settee. She was chain smoking - as was obvious from the overflowing ashtray on the floor. Maggie wore an old fur coat; a scarf covered her dyed ginger locks. There was no heating on and her lounge was bitterly cold. Old newspapers littered the floor.

Our hostess sighed:

- *"So you have brought your friend along. It's no use: I am going to jump out of the window. You can't stop me".*

Kay pleaded: - "Don't do it, Maggie! There are better times ahead, you'll see".

Maggie persisted: - "No, it's no use: I have made up my mind and am going to jump out of the window".

Walking over to the French windows I opened them wide:

- *"Come on, get on with it then. Just jump and stop wasting my time".*

Maggie's mouth dropped open with surprise. She was speechless. Kay looked horrified. ("How COULD you, Muriel?")

But I insisted: "Will you please hurry up. It's draughty and we are going to catch a cold because of you."

The woman's voice became hesitant: - "Well, I don't know"...

- *"Look, are you going to jump, yes or no? And, by the way, have you arranged for someone to pick up the mess downstairs afterwards? It's not fair to your neighbours".*

By now Maggie was giggling to cover her embarrassment. It was clear that she had no intention whatsoever of taking her own life. She was just lonely and seeking attention.

To be on the safe side I returned to check up on her regularly and also contacted the Social Services. Yes, she was on their list of patients and had enough money for food and heating.

This happened many years ago. Maggie is still alive and well. Now she has changed her tune to: - "How I wish I could die!"... (just in case someone else calls her bluff). She will live to a ripe old age, a totally selfcentred woman.

My spiritual work was taking up a lot of time. There was so much to learn, so many books to read! The more I read the more I realised that I knew nothing at all - which is, I suppose, the beginning of wisdom. My enquiring mind had a thirst for knowledge. I studied the beliefs of the North American Indians, the Kabbalah, philosophy, Magic etc. - in fact anything available and I attended various lectures. It's surprising just how many obscure societies there are in London!

However, I still made time to meditate most evenings. The power was now very strong in the room. I could almost hold it in my hand: a piece of Heaven. The minute I sat down, unseen kindly presences were already linking in with me. The room was so quiet... like the calm before the storm. What lay ahead?

And, sure enough, one of the strangest events of my life was about to take place...

What a pity I cannot meditate today on a regular basis because most of my clients arrive in the evening after work. My sons are now men who come and go, bring their friends along and stay up late watching television. Visitors pop in unexpectedly for a chat... One day I shall start all over again and who knows what will happen then...

So that particular evening started off as any other yet I had a strange feeling of expectancy, wondering what lay ahead. The atmosphere was very still, becoming gradually colder. Shivering I checked the thermostat... no, it was on 80. The central heating was doing its job. Yet the place grew even colder. Wrapping myself up in a cardigan I waited with a feeling of mounting uneasiness... Perhaps a cup of coffee would help... but instead I just sat there, transfixed while my heart started to beat very fast. Could it be fear? Looking back - no, I don't think so. It always seemed to happen when energy was being drawn from my solar plexus...

*To my left a faint rustling noise was now audible just behind the wall. Oh dear...
the sound was coming from between the settee and the window, growing
progressively louder until... all of a sudden it all happened... and I fell back in
total amazement!*

*A tall Native American had literally walked in through the wall. He turned
around in front of the television set and faced me. My mouth must have opened
and shut like a goldfish. He never moved and looked straight ahead in the
intensified silence. At that moment in time it was as though the whole world had
come to a standstill. Only his impressive headdress of large eagle feathers
swished gently in the stillness making the soft rustling noise heard earlier on.
Never had I seen a fully materialised spirit before and blinked to make sure it
was not a dream... no, this was the real thing. My previous ghostly visitors had
all been of the hologram type: a three dimensional moving picture superimposed
on top of the furniture in the room.*

*This, however, was totally different. The splendid Big Chief standing in front of
me with folded arms was made of flesh and blood. I could have reached out and
shaken his hand. He was bare chested, splendidly awesome and, with all the
feathers - Wow! What a presence. Now if this person were a product of my
imagination I would have expected a handsome Hollywood filmstar! In fact he
reminded me of the actor Victor Mature - a tanned, weatherbeaten version of him
with a large hooked nose. Traces of pockmarks were clearly visible on his skin.
My visitor was quite forbidding and had he said: "Boo!" to me I probably would
have run a mile. In the circumstances he never moved and remained silent -
which was just as well. (Don't suppose he spoke English anyhow.)*

*All of a sudden a scratching sound coming from behind the wall made me jump
and the Indian held out his hand waving someone else in. A plump woman
wrapped up in a blanket came scrambling in on all fours and crouched at his
feet. She too was middle aged and pockmarked. Her eyes were dark and fierce,
her hair plaited and oily - not at all my idea of a romantic Mini-Haha.*

*A few minutes later a young Brave came gliding in silently and stood behind the
woman. He was bare chested and had two or three feathers in his hair - a
pleasant enough chap, perhaps in his late twenties, with dimples in his cheeks.
But then, judging by the way he moved so swiftly and soundlessly, I would rather
be his friend than his enemy any day.*

*The trio never moved, only the rustling of feathers broke the silence. Junior,
unlike the two others, was more unsubstantial, so perhaps the power was running
out by the time he arrived making it impossible for him to materialise completely*

102

like the two others. However, he stood next to the Big Chief and behind the crouching woman - you'd think they were posing for a family photograph.

SO WHAT DO I DO NOW? What would John Wayne have done in the circumstances? He'd tilt his stetson back a little and hold up his begloved right hand, saying: "HOW!"...

So let's try that and see if it works. Standing up, I held up my right hand and called out: "HOW!"... (No this is not funny - you try it sometime). Still, there was no response so obviously none of them ever watch cowboy films. I added, hoping for the best: "God bless you friends, welcome!"
As there was nothing else to do to while away the time I took a closer look but didn't have the nerve to touch them: it was awesome enough being alone face to face with these proud warriors from another century. They stood in a bright light, every detail of their features clearly visible. The Big Chief wore a pale blue band across his forehead and arms so I gathered he must be my future Healing Guide popping in to introduce himself. (Spiritual Healing works with the help and cooperation of one of these Beings of Light and pale blue is the healing colour).

WHAT HAPPENS NEXT? Visitors from Heaven are a great honour but if they just stand motionless like statues one eventually runs out of conversation. I just couldn't carry on gawping at them forever nor ask, in true British fashion: "Would you like a cup of tea?" or: "What's the weather like in your part of the Next World?" As it was 1.30 a.m. I ventured: "God bless you, friends. It's wonderful meeting you but please go home now because I must go to bed". (And not: "Me heaps plenty honoured you come to my humble Tepee"...)

Success! No sooner had I pronounced these magic words than they all trooped out through the same place in the wall just as they had come in. So they must have picked my thoughts telepathically.

What an incredible experience! All very exciting once the event was safely over. Venturing into the kitchen I made a very welcome mug of coffee keeping all the lights on full! (Perhaps my visitors were still watching me...) By now the time was 2 o'clock. It took a while to calm my thoughts. Why do ordinary people like myself have these encounters? It seems to be a question of power building up in the room through meditation or perhaps, as has been suggested, I have the makings of a physical medium - the truth is that I really don't know, being as sceptical as the next. If anyone had told me that same story I would have giggled: "Go on. Pull the other"!

Years later, a medium told me:

"I have a Native American here. He says he came to introduce himself to you once. He is laughing and wants you to know he was your father in one of your previous incarnations. As a child, you were such fun, making him laugh. You would run out and play with wild animals. He'd be quite worried but they never harmed you. Your name was 'Talloolah' - 'Running Water' - because you never sat still. Now he has come back to help you with your work".

And, true enough, while giving healing I feel myself growing tall and powerful as the Spirit guide overshadows me. My arms become strong and muscled. The more I relax the greater the energy - a marvellous feeling, not frightening at all.

More recently a friend regressed me under hypnosis. First of all he talked me gently into relaxing. As I had known Frank for years I trusted him so just listened to the soothing sound of his voice and followed his instructions:

- "Do you remember when you were twelve years old? What happened then?" ... (Yes I recalled school, the teachers, the other girls)... Feeling more and more relaxed I heard his voice coaxing: "And, going further back in time.... you are five... What can you see?" (We were emigrating to Belgium. Everything seemed so grey and dismal)... By now comfortably drowsy I was nonetheless still aware of the room around me and a couple of friends watching. Although I had willingly submitted to this experiment I could still have opened my eyes at any time and snapped out of it. The voice continued:

- "You are feeling so relaxed and comfortable as you lay asleep in your mother's womb... so you're going further back in time, Muriel. Now you have become an adult again... standing up... outside in the fresh air. Can you see anything?"

At first... nothing. Just wind blowing in my face. Then tall trees started to appear... and a man entered my vision... Instant recognition: my Native American stood in the middle of the picture with a great welcoming grin on his face. This time I knew for certain he was my father - so obviously I must have been an Indian too. His hair was long and straight but he was not wearing any headdress. In the background beyond the trees I could see tepees and people going about their business... someone making a fire... smoke curling up... two women chatting... a man carrying a bundle of sticks: a peaceful village scene.

The next setting showed the Big Chief at the top of a mountain greeting the rising sun in all its glory. He was dancing while turning to face the four corners of the earth in turn. The large feathers of his headdress seemed transparent in the

104

dawn taking on the colours of the sky behind him: red, orange and pale blue - a magnificent sight.

Then we moved onto the following episode: the tepees on fire, people running away frantically from a shadow of invading men. After that the story becomes a blur... a vague feeling of being caught up in the massacre and raped but this did not bother me unduly as this time I was only an observer. It was a fascinating experiment although I could not relate emotionally to the story.

In the next scenario my father and I are alone in the mountain among the wild grass. He is fishing in a stream while I gather berries. There doesn't seem to be anyone else around so maybe we are the only two survivors. Did I eventually die in childbirth? The picture was becoming hazy and in the distance Frank's voice was calling me back...

Rubbing my eyes I looked around at the cosy room and decided it was great to be once more among my friends in the 20th century. With a big grin on his face my son Nathan was offering me a glass of white wine...

Reincarnation is a very interesting subject. It often explains why a person reacts in a specific way. Most people enjoy relaxing in front of an open fire in winter when the wind is howling outside. Even those with central heating still like to burn a log in the hearth. Whereas the vivacious young lady sitting in front of me explained how for some unknown reason the sight of flames made her go rigid with fear. The palms of her hands would turn clammy and she'd feel faint. I took a closer look at my sitter: Sharon was dressed in a flowery skirt and wore large hoop ear-rings. She'd also told me earlier on that she had a fascination for Wicca. The answer was obvious: in a previous life my sitter had been burnt at the stake as a witch. When I explained these simple facts to her the whole puzzle fitted into place and she was able to control her phobia.

Concentrating on another lady with thick auburn hair and green eyes I saw her clairvoyantly surrounded with hundreds of strange looking cats. "You were a priestess in a temple in Ancient Egypt... in charge of cats, some tame and others wild. People came and made offerings to these animals who were treated like gods".

- "How strange!", she replied, astonished: "I love cats and breed them. At the moment I have seven Abyssinian who are said to be the original descendants of the Egyptian ones". Coincidence?

Dozens of other similar cases spring to mind. With some people their previous life is obvious. If you feel an affinity with a country for no particular reason then the chances are you lived there in a previous life. For example, you decide to go to Rome on a holiday: you have never been there before and don't speak the language, yet the minute you arrive everything seems so familiar - it's like coming home. The chances are you were a Roman citizen in a previous incarnation.

Let's take another case. You are driving through Cornwall. At a cross-road you instinctively know there should be a pond in the vicinity. Yes! There it is... and further to the right the road leads to an inn. Sure enough a modern version of the "The Smuggler's Arms" stands exactly where you had visualised it. And slowly more hazy memories come flooding back.

These experiences could happen to anyone. The story becomes interesting when the person is also able provide names and correct information which he or she could not possibly know in ordinary circumstances.

It has been an interesting experiment for me to help a few friends go back in time by making them imagine they are going on a country walk through meadows full of flowers on a sunny day. This exercise clears their mind sufficiently for them to recall a previous life. They are neither hypnotised nor in a trance - simply totally calm. It is surprising what the brain can remember once all the stress has been set aside.

If life consists of three score plus ten before the final curtain then it has little purpose. But when you realise that you are in fact picking up the threads of a previous existence then everything starts to make sense. The principle revolves around the universal laws of cause and effect - or Karma: every action engenders a reaction. No angry God up there in Heaven is going to punish you for your sins. You punish yourself - or man will if you get caught.

Life can be compared to a pair of scales: on the one side there is good and on the other evil. If you have made a mistake, the scales will tilt towards the negative. So go out of your way to do something good and the balance will be restored. Karma can be carried down through various incarnations until, having learnt all life's lessons, you don't have to return anymore. Well, that's the theory anyway. So it's a good idea to achieve something worthwhile while you are here.

But back to my story, one month later. After an hour of meditation I was wonderfully relaxed. My whole body was tingling with electricity similar to the buzz one feels after physical exercise. Imaginary cobwebs seemed to be settling on top of my face making me want to brush them away. However, I knew this was Spirit drawing close, overshadowing me. Once again I was on the threshold of another world...

On an impulse I picked up a colouring pencil and a pad of paper from the coffee table. Now let's see... What was the purpose of this new experiment? Not being one of the world's most accomplished artists I started to doodle but almost immediately the pencil appeared to take on a life of its own and began to sketch flowers, more flowers, nothing but flowers at an increasing pace ... reminding me of my friend Gwyneira's automatic writing... but this was automatic floristry with a vengeance! I filled page after page at the speed of lightning, unable to stop. It was like driving a car without brakes down a mountain pass. At the same time the room became gradually colder and colder. My heart was racing... ectoplasm was being drawn from my solar plexus and pumped out into the room.

Finally, the drawings came to an abrupt stop and my hand was released. Maybe I had run out of petrol! All those flowers... Gratefully I massaged my aching wrist and inspected the pictures: every bunch was a psychic drawing that could be interpreted symbolically - prophecies which have since all been fulfilled.

However, the room remained freezing cold. My home was strangely silent as though life itself had been put on "Pause". "Oh, dear! This is only the first course", I thought uneasily. "What is going to happen next?" Was my Native American going to reappear in full regalia? Why, it was only a few weeks earlier that he had walked in through the solid wall to my left. But no, one visit was surely enough. What then? It was obvious that something was brewing. Why else did they require so much of my energy? The time was already well past midnight, but sleep was remote from my thoughts. Let's just wait and watch... No late night film had ever been so enthralling as this real life story.

Pensively I observed the corner near the curtains... Nothing...

But hold on, WHAT WAS THAT? Mist was slowly building up. Holding my breath I noticed small lights, the size of a hand, appearing one by one in mid-air. There were perhaps a dozen or so - I was too dumfounded to count them. Upon closer inspection I realised that they were flames - reminding me of an advertisement for British Gas - but what was their purpose? Then the penny dropped. Tongues of Fire, of course! That is what they were. Easter... Pentecost... According to the Gospels the Disciples had seen Tongues of Fire when the Holy Ghost had descended upon them. What other explanation could there be? I'd always taken these stories with a pinch of salt as they happened so long ago. Besides it wasn't even that time of the year. (But then who knows because our present-day calendar did not exist in Biblical times...)

Puzzled I wondered: "What has this to do with me anyhow? I am certainly not going to preach the Gospels to the four corners of the earth. All the mess Christians made killing each other through the centuries... Just leave me out!" No, you wouldn't see me in a million years standing outside a supermarket calling:

- "Hallelujah! Praise the Lord! Have you heard the Good News?"

At the back of my mind something was saying:

- "But what about Universal Love? Isn't that really what Jesus taught?"

- "Well, yes..."

- "And life after death? Didn't he prove that too? He talked to the spirits of Moses and Elijah..."

Hmm, I could see their point.

After what seemed like an eternity the flames slowly disappeared in the night. At this stage you'd think that was enough excitement for one evening. But no. I remained glued to the settee, still waiting, alert to the slightest movement in the room. The flames had only been an introduction... More was yet to come, that was for sure!

Try and relate this story to the average person - like me for instance before the event - and see them looking at you concernedly:

- "Perhaps you work too hard, dear. Why don't you take a rest?". (Or, to be more precise, what they really mean is: "Go and see a psychiatrist. You have a screw loose").

The time on the wall clock was 1.15 a.m. How on earth was I going to get up on time in the morning? Something was making me stay put, hardly daring to breathe... The room still felt freezing cold, even though the central heating was on full... (Thank goodness I was wearing my warm blue Winter dressing gown. What a ludicrous situation, entertaining spirits in my nightdress...)

108

Tension was mounting slowly but surely. (Well, you're asking for it, Muriel, so now don't complain.) Was that a faint fluttering sound? No.... YES!... So where was it coming from? From the same place to my left near the window, of course... However, the flapping, slightly louder now, was emanating from the ceiling. Was it Big Chief after all? But surely he couldn't be up there near the pelmet... unless he had a parachute... or wings, yes WINGS, that was definitely the sound I could hear - and they were flapping rhythmically. It must be a large bird: maybe he had brought his pet eagle along... oh, dear, what have I let myself in for? Restlessly I stared at the wall and waited... until all of a sudden...

W H O O S H!!

A giant white bird came flying in towards me. Instinctively I ducked while jumping forward out of its way as it hovered over the settee where I had been seated.

Getting up I turned around and looked at this amazing creature. It was E N O R M O U S! How can one attempt to describe something so strange? It was certainly as long as my fourseater settee and now remained still with only its wings flapping gently. This bird was a giant dove. There seemed to be a hole in the ceiling beyond which I could see its head with alert little dark eyes. No, I was not dreaming! If it had been imagination at least I would have expected something of average size, not this colossus. Such creatures only exist in fairy tales and legends... The Voyages of Sinbad... Joseph and the Argonaut-what-have-you... (Oh, why was my mind going blank as I tried to remember all those far-fetched tales?...)

On the dove's head was a golden crown encrusted with outsize rubies, pearls and sapphires, surmounted by a large cross of light. Never had I seen precious stones that size! In the subdued light the effect was dazzling. It would have been possible to stroke its white wings - but as the dove was larger than an eagle I was certainly not going to try it out! If its head was beyond the ceiling I reasoned that it must be partly materialised but the rest was spirit...

The HOLY SPIRIT! That's it!... (Oh, no! Don't be ridiculous, woman).

In all the Renaissance paintings the Holy Ghost was depicted as a modest dove of normal size. Was it perhaps a thought-form that had come to life? (i.e. people have believed in this Dove of Peace for so long that unwittingly they had actually built its form on the Astral). My feathered guest was alive and well aware of me too.

When I greeted it kindly its eyes turned and looked at me. On an impulse I added tactlessly (and could have kicked myself afterwards for saying it):

- "Sorry, but I don't believe in birds like you".

Yet, why was I not afraid? Because the atmosphere was so tranquil, the apparition seemed tame and gentle, emanating a feeling of serenity. In that instant in time a little of Heaven had come down to earth unexpectedly enveloping me in its mantle of light - an absolutely marvellous experience. Nothing seemed important anymore except this incredible giant Dove radiating love.

WHAT DO I DO NOW?

My nocturnal guest just carried on softly flapping its wings in the silence. This was incredible - but why me, just an ordinary person - I am no Joan of Arc. How does one deal with such a situation? No book of etiquette states how one should address the Holy Spirit. As with my previous visitor, the Native American, conversation was totally one-sided. So I just stood there happily watching it. The energy in the room was powerful, overwhelmingly good, relaxed and peaceful.

In the end I called: "Good-night, friend. God bless you. Thank you for coming: it's a great honour. Unfortunately I must go to bed now as it's very late and I have two children to look after in the morning". (What else could I have said? Any better ideas?)

The bird looked at me and I just had the feeling that although it had understood my message telepathically, yet it was reluctant to leave. It started to head away slowly, then hesitated and came back, looked at me again and, after a pause, stretched its large wings and flew away through the ceiling.

Strangely enough, after his departure, the room remained cold, charged with energy as though the next episode was just around the corner - or rather the other side of the wall.

But I CAN'T CARRY ON WATCHING ALL NIGHT!

It's okay for those who are able to sleep till lunchtime. Spirit obviously have no sense of time. (Sorry but the rest will have to wait until the next episode). Phew! Let's hope that's that. Did I do the right thing sending my guest back to the Next World? Should I now feel guilty? But, blow I AM EXHAUSTED!

110

Gratefully I sank into bed. What a night! (And my neighbour's husband who thinks I am a bored and lonely housewife...) Barely had my head touched the pillow than the alarm clock rang shrilly through my dreams, waking me up with a jerk. Not 7.30 already! Bleary-eyed I stretched, yawned and sat up in bed.

Another dull, wet, rainy winter morning. Wellies and umbrella today! In the next bedroom nothing stirred yet: the two boys were still fast asleep. Well, let's go and put the kettle on. A mug of hot coffee would clear my thoughts. The previous evening's events seemed remote in the clear daylight. Maybe I had dreamed them all.. An outsize Holy Ghost... whatever next!

But suddenly I jumped up, wide awake!

W H O O S H!!

The great Dove was back! With a clear swoop and beating of wings it was now entering my bedroom.

Ouch, no, it had not been a dream after all! The large bird was very much alive as it towered above the bed. "And it's not the end of the story either!" I thought, slightly alarmed. (My room is situated just behind the dining-room so that it's the same wall seen from the other side. And the bird was flying in from exactly the same spot near the ceiling.) There must have been a lot of power left in the dining-room for the Dove to be able to materialise first thing in the morning.

- "There goes my coffee and the boys' breakfast. They are going to be late" was all I could think of in my ridiculously practical way...

BUT THIS IS A UNIQUE EXPERIENCE, never to be repeated in your life! It's strange that in a crisis I should always think of mundane things - probably my way of trying to remain rational instead of panicking. However, my mind was in a turmoil as I never expected Spirit to appear at breakfast time when I am in a rush.

The bird was now hovering dangerously close to the top of my head, its large wings flapping rhythmically when, all of a sudden, it flew away again back through the same place in the wall, as silently as it had come in.

Maybe it is checking whether I am still there!

Hold on! What's happening NOW? In front of me in the right corner of the bedroom a cloud of silvery grey fog was curling up into the shape of a screen,

Rivetted, I watched as it lifted a little and then settled. A blurred picture was slowly coming into focus... yes, there was a sort of scaffolding seen from a side angle... Three men were hanging...

(Oh, here we go again... Can't blame it on cocaine, Muriel, you wouldn't even recognise the stuff if you saw it.) I felt quite vulnerable sitting up in bed with dishevelled hair watching a Biblical scene slowly coming to life.

The person in the centre was drawing me like a magnet - the only one to become clear to my eyes... it MUST be... it HAD to be... Jesus on the cross... with the crown of thorns on his head. He seemed small and undernourished - probably just over 5' tall - with dark hair, a swarthy complexion and a small, wispy beard. His head was hanging on his shoulder.

Oh, has he died already? Maybe not... Just drugged to kill the pain... Let's see... (Am I going barmy, by the way? Here, from my 20th century bed, I am frantically thinking of how best to administer first aid to Christ on the Cross... who died nearly 2,000 years ago). It's difficult to remain cool when faced with such an incredible sequence of events).

At the foot of the cross shabbily dressed Roman soldiers were asleep, some squatting, propped up against the scaffolding or each other, still hugging their swords. It must have been early morning for them too for one soldier was stretching and yawning in the misty dawn.

Very slowly Jesus lifted his head as I looked on helplessly: there was nothing I could do at this stage to help alleviate the pain. He opened his dark piercing eyes and looked straight at me. Our gaze met and interlocked for a fraction of a second... for some reason he seemed to recognise me... and then his head fell back on his shoulder once more.

In utter amazement I rubbed my head thinking aloud: - "Why me?"

And the reply came almost immediately: - "And why not you?"

It was all over. The picture across the room was gradually fading away. In a daze, I got up, opened the curtains to let in the cheerless winter morning. The milk float was rattling down the road. A neighbour couldn't start his car but persevered endlessly. And there was our friendly postman on his way. An elderly lady was walking her dog: they both looked incredibly alike.

112

Still perplexed, I padded into the kitchen while putting on my blue dressing-down. Eight o'clock. They'd probably still make it to school just in time...

After reading this chapter my friend Philip declared:

- "You can just about make me swallow the story of the bird but when it comes to Jesus on the Cross as well... ugh! it's just too much. You have a powerful imagination... the whole thing makes me feel uneasy. Stories like that don't happen to ordinary people."

The average person would agree wholeheartedly with his criticism - and so, probably, would I if it hadn't happened to me. Philip knew very well that I was telling the truth. But his mind just couldn't accept stories that upset his established protestant background.

In days gone by people believed the earth was flat and that one could fall off its edges. (There is still a Flat Earth Society in existence today). Through the centuries philosophers, mathematicians and astronomers have been derided or executed when they disturbed an established concept.

In my opinion the purpose of making me draw flowers at a fast pace was to build up extra energy so that I could see:

1) The Tongues of Fire (a picture in time);

2) The materialisation of the Dove, a powerful presence who came to introduce:

3) Jesus on the Cross (another image in time).

Both the Tongues of Fire and the Crucifixion were probably pages from the Akashic Records. (I am no scientist but if pictures travel at the speed of light then it should be possible to channel into them at a later stage).

Why should ordinary people have visions while others are not so fortunate? Probably because a) they are receptive in the first place, b) they take time to be still and c) they won't be petrified. It would be difficult for the average commuter rushing off to work in the morning to see a spirit coming down the escalator in the Underground. The person is so preoccupied with mundane matters that he wouldn't notice anyway. So, the conditions are not right.

In a rural area a shepherdess, for example, who is in tune with nature, could much more easily see an apparition.

Bernadette Soubirous was a French country girl. She lived in unsalubrious surroundings and had asthma. One winter morning while she was out picking sticks near a grotto she saw the spirit of a young lady in white who spoke to her. The girl rushed back home to tell her family who, being rather superstitious and afraid, refused to believe her story.

Bernadette was reprimanded and severely punished while the local clergy and authorities hummed and ha-ed over her fate. The outcome of this story is the present day pilgrimage centre. In the meantime the girl's life was ruined as she did not fit into her society anymore. Everywhere she went crowds of pilgrims followed her. She had become a prize exhibit. It couldn't have done her asthma nor her nerves much good. So eventually she became a nun and died at the age of 32.

Unwittingly, she had contributed to the Roman Catholic Church's prosperity who, after tormenting her for so long, then changed their minds and turned her into a saint. What a price to pay for seeing an apparition! Why didn't they just leave Bernadette alone? She could so easily have led a normal life and lived to see her great grandchildren.

The Gregorian calendar is full of names of obscure saints, most of whom were tortured to death. Joan of Arc heard voices too.
She was burnt at the stake and then canonised posthumously. Nowadays she would be put on tranquilisers.

Many people have been aware of an unseen presence around them at some stage in their life. Perhaps they were in a crisis and help arrived unexpectedly from the Next World. Afterwards they thought things over rationally and dismissed the event as a figment of their imagination because it made them feel uneasy.

Spiritual energy can build up anywhere in any religion. No one has the monopoly. In Flanders there is a village called "Lourdes" where pilgrims come and pray at an artificial grotto, telling their rosary beads with fervour while hoping for a miracle. A crude effigy of the Virgin Mary looks down benignly from the wall. A life-size statue of a squinting Bernadette is seen praying in front of the altar. Around her, crutches and walking sticks donated by various grateful patients complete the decor.

Yet Jesus said: "When two or three are gathered in my name I shall be in their midst". So, in actual fact, it did not matter whether that village had set itself up in competition with the original Lourdes. Pilgrims came trustingly, lit candles and said prayers. And slowly a healing energy started to build up - powerful enough to effect cures and miracles.

Now as far as mediums are concerned it's a different story altogether. All of them have been through the mill and as a result are more tolerant and understanding than the average person. They are ordinary sensitive people who have had at least one wonderful spiritual experience powerful enough to change their life. They have acquired a joyful inner awareness because they know for a fact that there is life after death. But clairvoyants are certainly not 'Holier than Thou' and enjoy a laugh and a joke as much as anyone else. After years of training these people become a channel for relaying messages from another dimension, just like a radio station. And at the same time some of the 'other wordly' spirituality has rubbed off on them bringing out the best in their personality. Once the door is open they can take a peep too. It's one of the perks of the job.

Mediumship is a serious vocation requiring total dedication. The work entails conducting services, giving public demonstrations of clairvoyance, private readings and generally listening, counselling, helping and cheering up others. It is very demanding. The phone can ring at any time of the day or night. Many are also healers: the two go together. A true medium is never well off as much of his or her work is unpaid and he or she can usually just make ends meet.

Sceptics will ridicule them demanding an instant vision too if they are to be believed at all. The answer is: start in humility at the end of the queue and work your way up. If you are sincere and receptive enough you too may eventually become a professional medium. And once you've made it don't expect gratitude! Occasionally someone may say "Thank you, you've been a great help" - but that's a bonus.

If you light a candle in the darkness it will attract those who will be delighted to snuff it out.

Chapter Nine

It was early morning and I was in the middle of a lovely deep sleep when suddenly the phone jerked me back to reality as it rang imperatively in the hall. Still in a daze I answered. A woman with a West Indian voice snapped:

- "Trisha!"

- "Er?... no, sorry, you have the wrong number". Yawning, I put the phone down and returned to bed. However, it was impossible to go back to sleep and in the end I got up.

The following morning at the same time, the phone woke me up again:

- "Is that you, Trisha?"

- "No, sorry, wrong number again. Would you like me to look up the name in the Telephone Directory?"

- "You ARE Trisha, don't LIE to me, and it's YOUR number I want!" (She was becoming angry).

- "Sorry, love, there is no Trisha here, my name is Muriel".

- "Then GO AND GET HER!" she screamed.

Now at this stage I could have told her where to go herself and slammed the phone down. But courtesy prevailed:

- "Look I don't know Trisha - never heard of her. Would you like to speak to my son instead? He lives here but his name is not Trisha".

- "So why did you phone at 7 then?"

- "Who, me? You must be joking. You've just got me out of bed".

- "You DID phone at 7 and spoke to my husband. What for? What did you say to him?" (She was furious.)

- "Your husband? Me? No, dear. Don't know you. You are obviously mistaken. Look. I am tired and am going to have a cup of coffee as you have woken me up yet again". Then I put the phone down.

Ten minutes later she rang once more:

- "Look, you ARE Trisha, aren't you? Admit it!"

- "NO! Don't even know you have a husband and if you do, good luck to you. I have enough on my plate without worrying about your husband - who is probably young enough to be my son anyway. He is all yours, dear." (Now why am I so patient?)

- "I have just received my phone bill and your number is there. On the 6th of August Delroy made a phone call to you. I DEMAND to know why! (She was screaming again).

- "It's quite possible, lots of men phone me as I am a medium".

- "Then give me your address and I am coming to see you NOW!"

- "No, you don't, you are obviously under stress. Phone me later when you've calmed down. I have a busy day ahead. Goodbye".

An hour later, she was on the phone yet again. This time, her voice was more subdued: - "Suppose I owe you an apology... it was me who came to see you at that date... not him. Remember you now. Look, can you help me? I suspect my husband of having an affair..."

- "With a person called Trisha. Don't remind me. Well, that should put your mind at rest: it isn't me!"

- "Do you think it's a good idea to phone this woman and threaten her?"

- "No, certainly not".

- "Let me tell you all about it"... (Oh, don't! Can't face it).

Why didn't she confront her husband instead of accusing me? As far as I am concerned she is welcome to Delroy and he to her.
Never a dull moment for a medium.

Brother Stanley, a great character who would often allow his Zulu spirit guide to take him over. Chief Zamba had been decapitated in 1866. Thankfully I saw him complete with his head! Although an awe-inspiring presence, he was also immensely likeable. I was to encourage him to pronounce new words - now who has ever taught English conversation to a ghost?....

Brother Stanley and Zamba

*On an impulse I decided to go and visit another Spiritualist Church in my area.
"It's informal and friendly" a friend assured me.*

*There was a healing session on that afternoon, the sun was shining, and so I set
off just after lunch. The place wasn't difficult to find either - an imposing
Victorian house with "MORDEN SPIRITUALIST CHURCH" written in bold
letters on its facade - just in case I had any doubts. The door was on the latch
and I went in.*

*In front of me carpeted stairs led to the first floor. On my right through open
doors I saw the church with its neat rows of chairs bathed in the sunshine. The
rostrum was decorated with flowers. As the place seemed empty I walked up the
stairs. Suddenly, a door opened and Brother Stanley came out: a tall, well
dressed man with white hair, a black velvet jacket, pressed trousers and a large
crucifix hanging on his stomach.*

*At first he frowned, puzzled as he looked at me and then a large smile lit up his
face. He came forward and shook hands, greeting me warmly like a long lost
friend:*

*- "Ah, so you have come at last! Spirit have predicted your arrival for sometime
now. I desperately need someone to help me run this church.".*

Staring at him, open mouthed, I muttered:

- "Err... I beg your pardon?"

*- "Don't tell me you have come for healing! You are early but in a short while
patients will be here queuing up for treatment and I could do with your
assistance on a regular basis every Thursday afternoon. Now come along. Let
me show you the office..." (He never asked: "Would it be convenient? Can you
spare the time?" He simply took it for granted that Spirit had sent me and that
was that). He led me to a small and tidy room with an oak desk, religious
pictures on the wall and again an assortment of flowers in pots and vases. The
atmosphere was pleasant and serene. Instinctively I looked over my shoulder
feeling that unseen presences were watching me.*

*And so I started working at the church and would remain there for several years.
Often I would be alone in the house but it never felt empty. The place seemed to
have a life of its own. Footsteps would be heard walking down the stairs... I'd go*

South African plain

and see who was there but no... no one... However, the ghost must have been a smoker judging by the strong smell of tobacco he'd left behind in the hall.

Stan would shrug: "Oh, that's the spirit of the old president keeping an eye on the place - nothing to worry about. He smoked a pipe, by the way." (Now why hadn't I guessed?)

From time to time I would be talking to someone in the office when we'd both hear the voices of people having a lively conversation in the church when no one else was in the house.

Once I heard loud chatting and laughing going on inside the sanctuary, the same sort of noise one would expect in a pub... When I opened the door the conversations stopped abruptly and yes... the room was empty.

Brother Stanley was a friendly, relaxed man, easy to get on with: on the one hand a down-to-earth cockney full of fun and laughter and on the other a very spiritual, almost holy person - all rolled into one. His enthusiasm was infectious.

Stan was a born salesman. At the church jumble sales he would greet a visitor - who was not even particularly interested in buying anything - and within a matter of minutes and general merriment off she would go clutching say, an old saucepan, delighted at having acquired such a bargain.

My friend kissed all the ladies: young ones and old grannies alike were given a hug - in his books it was only friendship and never implied anything improper - all part of the service.

Over the following months I accompanied him around numerous hospital wards as he made everyone laugh, including the staff - a wonderfully gifted man. He chatted to the very sick and by the time he left the patient would be giggling away merrily, feeling ten times better. A breath of fresh air, was Stan. On many occasions he would listen for hours in total concentration to elderly people's troubles, tears of sympathy welling in his eyes.

When this medium conducted a service his clairvoyance was great showmanship, the congregation in fits of laughter. The evidence, however, was spot on. His favourite irreverent quote was: "You can kiss a nun once, you can kiss a nun twice, but you mustn't get into the habit" - and some of the elderly ladies were horrified! Yet when he said the Opening Prayer it was with great fervour and sincerity, his personality becoming serious and spiritual.

Every service is taken by a different medium. Most clairvoyants give a good demonstration but from time to time the odd one is boring and should have retired ages ago. These are recruited at the last minute when the medium for the evening can't turn up. After giving healing before the service, I would slip in quietly and sit next to Stan at the rear of the church. Now when the poor medium happened to be one of those dreary ones, droning on and on endlessly, lulling the congregation to sleep, Stan would become restless and whisper witty schoolboy remarks that were so funny I was choking with suppressed laughter. In the silence my giggles were magnified and soon people would turn around, frowning in disgust: "Shhh...." which made it even worse.

Stan threw me in at the deep end. I was still so unsure of myself!

- "Go on, Muriel, the medium can't come - you take the service. Don't panic. I'll carry on with the healing session in the sanctuary. Just call if you need help".

And there I was, within a matter of minutes, my heart pounding, standing in front of a sea of faces - not all of them sympathetic.

- "If anyone can do a better job, they are welcome to take over and I shall gladly sit down", I announced. Nobody moved.

It was invaluable experience addressing an audience. Most of the people were very understanding:

- "It's fine, don't worry. Just carry on".

Occasionally you'd get the odd one who would gleefully rub his hands together:

- "Ha-Ha! We have an inexperienced one here. Let's see if I can make her lose her nerve".

You may leave a rostrum walking on thin air but equally you can be made to feel so small you would gladly crawl away under the carpet. But today, thankfully, I can cope with these situations. The last time a member of a congregation tried to ridicule me I managed to turn the joke on him. Furious, he got up and stormed out of the church to a round of applause from the delighted audience.

Stan took over where my teacher Bill left off. He treated me like a mature professional medium and healer (which I certainly was not!) and gave me total freedom of the church.

- *"You want to change something? Great! Let's hear your idea".*

(Major decisions, of course had to be discussed at the committee meetings). There was little time for anything else in my life: I could have moved in with a sleeping bag. Always a flow of people would come along with their problems and their aches and pains. As this was all voluntary work it did not pay my bills. Some patients were happy with the help they received while others criticised and complained. But nothing worried Stanley. He was always cheerful, seeing the silver lining around any dark cloud. He had a tremendous amount of faith:

- *"If you have a problem, just look at it squarely and you will find a solution. Then it will cease to be a problem. Someone up there is looking after you".*

Now we come to the strange part of my story. The war had left this man in a wheelchair, paralysed with an injured spine. After lengthy hospital treatment the doctors declared they could not help him anymore. And one day he met a healer, an old lady, who over a matter of months, cured his spine trouble and got him back on his feet again:

- *"I was so grateful, I vowed to become a healer and spend the rest of my life helping others" Stan would recall.*

On one of those busy afternoons before the arrival of the flow of patients Stanley turned to me:

- *"Let's go into the sanctuary and meditate".*

- *"Fine" I replied.*

On this particular occasion we both sat on a chair facing each other. The weather outside was overcast and dull. Stan seemed to doze off, slouching on the seat. Within a matter of seconds he began to breathe heavily. Rivetted I watched as the breathing became deeper. The man seemed to have lost consciousness altogether. Then he started to redress himself as, puffing away, he pushed the chair aside with one almighty sweep and stood up, very tall, beating his chest with clenched fists. By this time Stan appeared about seven foot tall, almost touching the ceiling. Upon closer inspection I observed a shadow on top of him of that size.

- *"MMMM..... MMMMMMMM...." a strange deep voice bellowed.*

" - MMMMM.... Me Z-A-M-B-A!... Good here! Mmmmm..."

Unperturbed I answered:

- "Hi, Zamba! Welcome. God bless you."

By now it was obvious that the entity was as curious to meet me as I was to see him... But he was struggling for words and I realised he could not speak English.

- "Me, MURIEL!" I encouraged him, beating my own chest.

- "MMMM... Hmmmm... Moo...well" he smiled with appreciation of my efforts and carried on talking excitedly in his own language.

Then, suddenly I saw him, clearly outlined in the gathering dusk: the shadow who had taken over Stan belonged to a majestic Zulu warrior in full regalia complete with a leopard skin across his torso and a bunch of black and white feathers on top of his head. Now why didn't I feel frightened? Because he radiated such warmth and kindness...

Zamba did not stay long. The power was already running out. Slowly Stan's breathing was coming back to normal. The Zulu was fading away...

Having progressively shrunken back to his normal size, Stan returned to life. Rubbing his eyes he blinked in astonishment and then exercised his aching neck:

- "Oh, my neck... I say, what happened?" he asked in a daze. "Did you meet Zamba?"

Regaining consciousness, the poor chap was now aching all over... the ghost had stretched his body when he'd borrowed it.

- "Yes, we've just had a chat!" I answered with a smile. "And I tell you what: he's really nice. If you could go off again sometime I'll try and get more information from him."

Couldn't wait! Why is it that in my humdrum life when occasionally something does happen it is always mega size? Zamba was the Spirit Guide who worked through Stan, taking his body over in order to heal a steady flow of patients. Thanks to the Zulu's help he managed to work very hard without feeling exhausted. It was strange assisting the ghost of an African tribesman! When Stan gave healing he seemed to grow twice his size, taking on a different personality altogether: here was a gentle but authoritative Zulu chief. The patient could not see the spirit but certainly felt his powerful presence.

124

No one had ever encouraged Zamba to talk before and he was delighted at having found a new friend:

- "Hmmmm.... MMMMMM.... Good here! GOOD HERE!" he would introduce himself banging his fists on his chest.

- "Me ZAMBA!... HMMMMM....

(You'd think he was Tarzan the way he acted).

- "Yes, okay, Zamba. It IS good here. Lovely to see you again..." I would smile encouragingly, resisting the temptation to say: "Me Jane". "My name is Muriel! Me-oo-reeell".

- "Moo-well!" he repeated, giggling with merriment.

Laughing I looked up at this enormous Zulu chief towering above me. He was such a nice chap.

Another time Zamba patted me on the head: "Good... good little one... come and help my instrument" (i.e. Stan). "Much.... MUCH WORK to be done".

- "Why, Zamba you can speak English. Good, VERY GOOD!"

Proudly, the spirit announced:

- "Zamba go to Halls of Learning... Big, BIG halls here... learn easy."

- "Oh, I understand: you mean that your brain is not limited by physical conditions and so you can remember much more easily..."

- "Yes. That's right, little one!..."

Suddenly he became very quiet as he bent forward putting his hand to his ear:

- "Sshh... listen, can you hear?"

(Trust me - I couldn't hear anything!) But the Zulu was now blowing softly through his fingers while whispering:

- "Husshh... Can you hear the wind... ssshhh.... the wind... the Wind of Peace"...

Standing up straight once more - almost reaching the ceiling - he held up his hand in a strangely majestic blessing:

- *"May the wind... THE WIND OF PEACE... BE WITH YOU ALL!"*

He was so sincere and endearing - yet at the same time awe inspiring.

Over the following months Zamba came back regularly. Progressively he started to use new phrases in English and was very pleased with himself. From time to time the guide could not pronounce a specific word and I would make him repeat it until he said it correctly, amidst peels of laughter on both sides. He was a great character and what an incongruous situation! How many people have ever taught English conversation to a ghost?

- *"Tell me a little about your life on earth, Zamba. What was your home like?*

He thought seriously for a moment then announced:

- *"Many,... MANY wild animals. God's creatures around me. Wonderful! Big spaces... BIG skies."*

- *"And did you bring your surroundings with you in the Next World? Can you see deer, elephants and lions around you now?"*

- *"Of course!"*

- *"Did you ever have a wife?"*

At this Zamba boasted joyfully:

- *"Me, not one but FOUR wives!"*

- *"Oh, that must have kept you busy! And are they there with you? Yes? Don't they ever argue? Aren't they jealous of each other?"*

- *"No, no. In Africa, it is our custom".*

- *"And so, with four wives, how many children did you produce?"*

He roared with laughter:

- *"Many... MANY children... Zamba can't count them all".*

126

He also confided that he had been decapitated in 1866 for helping a white missionary:

- "Ugh, that was horrible!" he shuddered, massaging the nape of his neck. "My head went rolling... just like THAT!" (This was illustrated with a sweep of the hand). "Now Zamba come back to help other religious men". (That explained why, after a trance session, Stan's neck felt so painful.)

So there I was having a lively conversation with a delightful Zulu chief (and a decapitated one at that) who had died well over a century ago. Fortunately my guest now showed himself complete with a head.

Stanley himself was not a great reader and knew almost nothing about Zamba's background. However, he did show me an apport - a little black and white vignette that had appeared from nowhere in his Absent Healing book (a book in which he wrote the names of patients requesting his healing thoughts). The small picture depicted a Zulu Chief brandishing a large oblong shield in one hand and a spear in the other. He was wearing a leopard skin across his chest. A bunch of black and white feathers crowning his head gave him a splendid, regal appearance. Underneath the name "ZAMBA" was clearly printed.

Being inquisitive I went to the Public Library and looked up the History of South Africa. Now if the Zulu had died in 1866 who would have been the leader at the time? Would he know? It would be an interesting experiment to find out how knowledgeable he was. 'Zamba'... Let's see... Was the name connected with 'Zambia'?... On the other hand as he could see all those animals then surely there was water nearby. So was his village situated near the Zambezi... Perhaps I should ask him about Shaka too. (At the time the film "Shaka" had not been made and very few people here had ever heard of the African tyrant's name - certainly not Stan). Not that I was an expert but still, it was worth a try.

So at our next meeting I asked the Spirit:

- "Did you live near the Zambezi?"

- "Zambezi? No! No! Not Zambezi. But: BEEZEE-BEEZEE! Yes, Zamba lived there!" (He was getting quite excited at the mention of a familiar word).

- "And did you know Shaka?"

At this, Zamba frowned and shuddered:

"He bad... BAD man.... ugh! Not Shaka but: TSHAKA-TSHAKA!

Now here was an interesting point. The following day I checked in a book and read: "Shaka.... also pronounced 'Tshaka' by the Zulus"…. Couldn't find 'Beezee' anywhere but it was a possibility. If Zamba only had four wives he was a local chief but probably not of national fame so I wouldn't find him in the History of South Africa.

On that particular Thursday Stan and I sat meditating in the sanctuary before another busy healing session. After ten minutes I opened my eyes and looked at my companion who seemed to have drifted off. Perhaps he had fallen asleep... But the deep, heavy breathing was now starting again while Stan remained dead to this world. Maybe Zamba was coming through. Great! Something to look forward to. But to my surprise instead of growing in stature Stan was slowly shrinking. How strange! What was going on? A powercut?... Ouch! What a situation... alone with an unconscious man waiting for one of Spirit's special surprises...

With mixed feelings I watched…. while the heavy breathing increased and my friend seemed to shrink even further.

Then silence...

The atmosphere felt somehow different too...

- "HEY!... I'm lost... It ain't half dark 'ere. Help!

H-E-L-P !!"

A little boy's whimpering voice was calling. Stan started rubbing his eyes and picking his nose - but of course it was the entity who had taken over his body. With amusement I watched him wiping his nose on Stan's plum velvet jacket.

- "H-E-L-P ! ! ! ! Can't see a bloody thing". (The little cockney spirit was now sobbing away in a state of panic.)

Remembering the Spiritualist formula for addressing ghosts I said:

- "God bless you, friend. What can I do to help you?"

- "BLIMEY! Is there someone there?" (More tears and sniffing). "Can't find my Mummy! Waaahh!"

- *"Come on now, calm down. Don't worry. I'll look after you. What's your name?"* (My motherly instincts made me hug him - and Stan - at the same time but as the latter was in a trance anyway he didn't comment. The situation was becoming quite ludicrous).

- *"I'm Basil"*...

- *"What year is it then? Tell me what has happened".*

- *"It's 1943, don't you know?... Just got knocked down by this army lorry, see... It's this bleedin' war. Oh, my poor head..."* (He was now holding his head with both hands and rocking himself in agony).

- *"Basil, please stop sniffing for a minute and listen to me. My mind is going to project light towards you. Just be still and concentrate"*...

After a short pause I asked: *"Now look around: can you see a light anywhere, even a faint glow?"*

The boy's plaintive voice resumed: *"I've been here in the dark for a hell of a long time...er..."* (Suddenly his tone changed to one of excitement)... *"Hang on, blimey, yeah... I can just about see something there in the distance"....*

Another silence followed. Oh, dear! Didn't want to lose him at this stage... Uneasily I thought: *"Help! Give me some inspiration... What happens now?"*

- *"Basil! Can you hear me? Perhaps we could say the Lord's Prayer together. It will produce positive energy to lighten your path"*...

A faint little voice groaned: *"Dunno no prayers. Never been taught none, see"*...

- *"Well why don't you just try and repeat after me:* *"Our Father"*.... and I carried on saying the prayer, hoping for the best. At the first few words the boy shut his eyes and smiled contentedly:

- *"Oooh.... Oooh... it's wonderful. I can feel this heat coming all over me... cor blimey! It ain't half hot. Just carry on"...* (He reminded me of a purring cat).

Suddenly he sat up bold straight: *"Yeah! I can see the light! Carry on with the prayer, lady... I can see! Hurray!*

I CAN SEE !... And, hang on a minute...

I CAN SEE YOU TOO!"

Basil was jumping up and down on his seat with excitement.

Faintly I could now make out the outline of a little boy with a large cloth cap on his head and knee length shorts retained by braces. Incredible! He had probably been killed while crossing the road. The accident had damaged his brain and so Basil had remained in a state of shock, earthbound, ever since. That is, until Zamba who could not get through to him, decided that I may be able to help in redirecting him to the Spirit World. And it had worked!

After that Zamba would often let Basil come through and talk to me. The Zulu would search around calling:

- *"You coming?... Where are you now? Basil! You naughty boy!"*

In the ensuing silence while Stan went still deeper into trance I would hear Basil's voice calling from a distance:

- *"Oy... there! Muriel, mate. Wait for me!..."*

And suddenly Zamba would make way for the little Cockney who would come in joyfully imitating the Zulu's mannerisms, banging his chest with his fists:

- *"MMmmmm... Good here! GOOD HERE!... ME: BASIL! Ha-ha! Hey, listen. Guess what happened? Zamba just gave me a clip 'round the earhole. Told me to behave meself".*

- *"Hello, Basil. You seem very cheerful today. Have you found your mother yet?"*

- *"Oh, yeah. Met the rest of the family too. But I want to be with Zamba. More going on, see. 'Ere, I feel sorry for you lot over there. Better off over here, ha-ha! No, but, seriously we've got to send you all this healing, see. What with all the wars going on and that"...*

His tone was becoming preoccupied. What an odd mixture: a boisterous cockney boy, unchanged since his death in 1943 but with newly found maturity and wisdom acquired since his arrival in the Spirit World. It also struck me that Stan had a bit of both spirits' personality - probably when they came and overshadowed him. Yet Zamba and Basil were two distinct people in their own right.

130

- "Ere, must go now, Muriel, mate. Zamba's coming back".

Those were memorable afternoons. Eventually Stanley decided it was time to retire and move to Devon where he would carry on with his spiritual work.

On the last healing afternoon Zamba came through, patted me on the head and announced:

- "Mmmmm.... Good here.... GOOD HERE! Instrument now moving away. Basil happy in the Spirit World - also healing. Zamba watch him. Still much work... MUCH WORK to be done".

- "I shall miss you, dear Zamba. You have become my friend".

- "Little one must not be sad. Just call - anytime. Zamba come... (Showing the space between his eyebrows - the psychic eye): "You see in here... the elephants, the lions and... Zamba!"

The power was going. Zamba was slowly fading away... He whispered:

- "Zamba go now... God bless you... God bless"... G..."

Shortly afterwards Stan left the church. He had every confidence in my capabilities to run the place smoothly. It was very hard going. But I did my best. There are always the few who do the work and the others who tell them how to do it! It was all invaluable experience that built up my confidence both as a medium and as a healer. Gradually I became totally exhausted and had to let someone else take over when I went into hospital for a major operation.

Stan still lives in Devon today. Every Christmas I receive a bright and cheerful card signed: "With love from Bro Stanley and Zamba".

I shall never forget Stanley, Zamba and Basil, for together we had managed to establish a wonderful friendship beyond the boundaries of time.

As I reminisce all these years later remembering every detail, in my mind's eye I see long stretches of the African Veldt with a few bushes here and there, antelope, giraffe and elephants grazing peacefully....

There is a great buzz of excitement around me now as Spirit draws close, interested in my writing. Zamba's presence is definitely here, watching, smiling....

131

- "MMM... Good here,.... little one remembers"... while someone else nudges me in the ribs and I hear the distinct cockney voice once again:

- "Oy, Muriel mate, you'll never guess what: I am an 'ealer too now and I can spell!"...

As in a dream Zamba's voice whispers faintly: "Husshh... Sshhh... Can you hear... the wind... sshhh... the Wind of Peace..."

Echoes of those voices slowly fade away in the night until only the silence remains broken by the steady clicking of my word processor.

Life in the Spirit World

Zamba was a very useful source of information about everyday life in the Next World:

- "Can you see my spirit guide, the French sister-of-mercy?"

- "Yes, she here alright.

- "Can you talk to her, Zamba?"

- "No, she holy lady - just stand there silently - No talk to Zamba."

- "Then can you see my father or any other member of my family?"

The Zulu shrugged his shoulders:

- "No, not here. Different sphere."

The guide lived in a world of thought. In his mind he had taken his African scenery along because that is where he felt comfortable. No, there was no need for him to eat but he could do so if he wished. Again, it was sufficient for Zamba to visualise food and it would appear, rather than, say, having to peel vegetables and cook them in a pot.

Basil would even come through licking his fingers:

- "I am busy eating fish and chips out of a newspaper. Got them from the chippie down the road."

As stated earlier, astral travelling is an experience I have had on numerous occasions. For instance, I remember sailing into the Spirit World and going through a prairie full of tall, beautiful flowers. Their scent was wonderful. Ahead in the distance were snow-capped mountains. It was pleasantly warm, the landscape reminiscent of Canada. There were no wild animals nor insects and although the sky was blue I can't remember seeing the sun.

We live in a physical world i.e. if we wish to go from A to B we have to walk, using our feet. In the Next World you simply concentrate on your intended destination and, hey presto, there you are. So if spirits want to come back to visit someone on earth it is a relatively easy matter when they live in the realms nearest to ours but once they have progressed further it takes much more energy to do so.

When we speak we use our voice, over there it all happens telepathically - by thought transference. This is how clairvoyance is transmitted to a medium.

As there is no Time concept either, spirits can perceive both past and future events. Zamba warned me that he could see streets on fire in London in the near future - well before the riots occurred. Also that "Many... MANY people would die from a new disease" (Aids was still unheard of) but that eventually a cure would be found for it. However, this would be succeeded by another unknown illness for which there will be no remedy. (Oh, dear)...

So if Time does not exist over there then your body won't age either. In fact at death you go back to the period in your life when you were at your best. Wrinkles and illnesses simply disappear. The spirits of various friends have stood at the foot of my bed waving good-bye. They all looked splendid.

As you don't have to walk or run, consequently there are no sports, ball games, cars, trains nor aeroplanes. However, at a large football games on earth, those spirit people interested are watching in the front row! Ordinary physical jobs and skills are not required either. So you won't see the postman on his morning rounds nor hear the clatter of milk bottles, etc.

Halls of Learning are places where you can study anything you wish and as your brain is not restricted by physical limitations you learn very fast with little effort. (That is how Zamba learned English so quickly).

Don't think you will get bored, sitting on a pink cloud all day playing the harp because there is no shortage of work - whatever you would enjoy doing. One of the main jobs consists in helping people in the Spirit World or on earth. When, for example, 60 people die suddenly in an aeroplane disaster they feel completely disorientated, believing they are still alive. Ambulances arrive, doctors and nurses fuss over the bodies while these souls helplessly call out: "Hey, I am here! Can't you see me?" But no, the doctors don't respond and so they panic. Soon a reception committee from the Next Realms is at their side to offer reassurance and guide them safely away.

Just imagine listening to a concert conducted by Beethoven live! (I haven't worked out how the orchestra would play: using musical instruments or the power of thought.)

Those who die after a long illness are taken to the Halls of Rest. These are hospitals where newcomers remain for perhaps six months. They are not given any medicine but the whole building stands underneath a great blue healing light - sounds strange, doesn't it? And yet on several occasions I have floated through these wards. The patients were not aware of my presence.

The world we go to upon our death is the nearest to our physical plane so it still resembles the landscape we are used to otherwise newcomers would be in a state of shock. We may take along with us a mental replica of our homes and familiar possessions.

Regularly I have the same dream. Opening a door I enter a sitting room. It's my grandparents' home as I remember it. Grandfather is sitting near the fire engrossed in a copy of the 'Readers' Digest' while Gran is busy knitting. Our old tabby cat is curled up in the fireside chair. It all seems so peaceful. Grandad looks up briefly, nods in acknowledgement of my presence and carries on reading - as though I have only been gone a matter of minutes. The large oak table covered with a lace tablecloth... familiar paintings on the wall... they are all there. It seems as though time has stood still. Pottering about I feel happy until, reluctantly, it's time to wake up.

Love binds people (and their pets) in the Next World - not a wedding ring. What happens if you had two partners? You will be with both or with the one you loved best. What if you could not stand the sight of each other? Then you will wave from a distance but won't be together. You join a group of people on your own wavelength.

This reminds me of a message I gave in church to an elderly woman:

- "Your husband is here; he tells me his name is Fred and he died of cancer."

- "Yes, that's him alright! Will you tell him from me that he can go straight back to the Spirit World and stay there. I had to put up with him when he was alive and am certainly not going to tolerate him now. So just tell him to get lost!"

(She was angry, much to the congregation's amusement). But I persisted:

- "Fred says he DID care. He is talking about a diamond bracelet he gave you for your wedding anniversary."

She snapped: "Don't remind me. Ha! The famous diamond bracelet! Yes, he was always boasting about it, the bloody liar. Never bought me no bracelet. Spent all his money on the greyhounds."

This lady has since passed - she was a real battle-axe. Somehow I felt sorry for her husband notwithstanding all his shortcomings and just hope they are not reunited up there or Heaven would never be the same again.

There are many books describing life in the Next World but I can only tell you about my own experiences. What is the point of repeating what I have read elsewhere?

Once while meditating I sailed through a dark tunnel towards a blinding light. Right at the end several relatives stood smiling welcomingly but I turned around and came back through the tunnel. Recently, various people interviewed on television have described a near death experience whilst on the operating theatre. They claim to have floated through a dark tunnel towards a brilliant light at the end... yes, I can relate to that. Another time I came to a river in the countryside. On the other side across a bridge stood my grandparents waving at me. But I felt the time was not right and returned to my own physical body and front room.

The Spirit World seems to be a dimension where you earn your place through work on this earth. Some of my acquaintances are determined to buy their ticket to Heaven by going to church every Sunday (or mosque on a Friday etc.) To me, I am afraid it means very little: what you believe in is not that important but what you do about it is. In my books, (and I don't expect anyone to agree with me) a good atheist who goes out of his way to help others is more spiritual than a Sunday Christian who attends services regularly and only helps himself.

There are many planes in the Next World. One progresses slowly from one level to the next. The ultimate goal is Nirvana - a state of ultimate bliss or union with God, when one does not have to return to earth anymore. But in the meantime you have to pop back to experience new challenges and learn more lessons.

In the Middle Ages when soldiers went into battle they each carried a sealed letter written by the local bishop. It was addressed to St Peter and read something like this:

- "Dear St Peter,

"Please admit the holder of this permit into Heaven. We vouch that he is a fine Christian who regularly attends church."

I hope St Peter could read Latin.

Chapter Ten

You wouldn't believe the phone calls I receive! Some are quite funny too, for instance this one which I repeat ad verbatim:

- "Hello! Muriel? Neil here. I believe you left a message on my answering machine requesting my services." (He has a young, gentle but businesslike voice).

- "Who? Me? No, I didn't. Who are you and what services do you offer anyway?"

- "I am a male escort. I will come and give you a full massage and anything else you wish for £30. Although operating from home I am prepared to travel."

- "Wow! That's a bargain. So you are a male prostitute?"

- "If that is what you wish to call it."

- "Someone has played a trick on you, Neil, it's a hoax. I never left a message on your answering machine."

- "Please think it over", he persisted, "I charge extra for added services, of course, such as tying me up and whipping me."

 - "My husband would not approve."

- "Most of my clients are married women. I'll come in the afternoon when he is away."

- "Neil, I am old enough to be your mother. How old are you?"

- "I am 29 but that does not matter. My clients are your age upwards."

- "Don't you find it disgusting at times? Surely all your clients don't turn you on, in which case, what do you do: shut your eyes and think of England?"

Neil considered my remark very seriously:

- "Must admit that at times it's rather difficult... and some women can be very abusive."

- "Aren't you afraid of getting Aids?"

- "No. I am clean, discreet and always use a contraceptive."

- "Bet your mother doesn't know what you do! She would not be proud of you."

- "No, I don't tell her. Business has been rather slack over the past eight months."

- "It's the recession. Women can't afford sex anymore! But, tell me: do you pay V.A.T. every time you perform?" (I had visions of a meter being installed).

- "No, I don't."

- "Listen Neil. Occasionally men phone asking if I offer sex. Shall I give them your phone number?"

- "Well, I prefer women, really. Had a few experiences but didn't like them. By the way: what do you do for a living, Muriel?"

- "I am a medium."

- "Oh, great! Haven't had a reading for ten years. Tell you what: let's do a swap. You give me a reading and I'll give you a massage with - or without - extra services.

- "No, thanks all the same, Neil. You seem a very nice man - and since you are so good at massage why don't you study osteopathy? It's also massaging. You'd earn plenty of money doing something respectable. You can't expect to carry on performing at this rate in ten years' time."

- "Mmmm... that's not a bad idea at all. I'll think it over. But would you like my phone number, Muriel, in case you change your mind? Or maybe you know among your clients someone who may require my services?"

Poor Neil! Our chat brightened up my day. He never realised I was teasing him. However, I was concerned: a pleasant young man, my own son's age, choosing prostitution as a career - it was such a pity. Still, I did try and help by advising him to study something else but doubt whether he will listen. And what about married women who would take up such an offer? They are immediately open to blackmail by an unscrupulous male escort.

A Few Words on Witchcraft and Paganism

Modern Wicca - the Craft - is the practice of white witches who follow the old religion, communing with gods and goddesses and the forces of nature. They also make talismans and cast good spells to help themselves and others. (In this context "white" refers to White Magic and the Light - as opposed to "Black Magic" and the forces of Darkness.)

Spells

A spell does not necessarily belong to the realm of fairy tales. If prepared according to rules and regulations it can be effective. However, a request must be reasonable, and not against the Laws of the Universe. For example, if you ask for your partner to be protected from danger and come home safely (supposing he is a soldier) - this is a valid request. But it is wrong to ask that the man you like split up with his wife because in so doing you are interfering with his freewill.

You can't send negative thoughts to others because they will come back to you and you won't prosper. Magical spells call up powerful forces from another dimension. They have to be performed correctly or you could be in serious trouble. So, as in clairvoyance, if you are not sure - leave well alone.

In the past, witches were blamed for the plague and other calamities, as were Jews and Gypsies. No one ever gave them a fair chance. They were a convenient scapegoat for an ignorant society.

An elderly woman who lived alone with her cat would immediately be accused of cohorting with the Devil - the animal was regarded as a demon who assisted her in her evil spells. It never occurred to her neighbours that the old lady was simply lonely and glad for the little creature's friendship.

Witches, Pagans, Druids etc. simply celebrate the passing of the seasons and the fertility of the land. But the Church condemned all competition while incorporating these same rituals in her own festivities.

Christmas comes at the Winter Solstice - the longest night of the year. So the old traditions were conveniently adapted to celebrate the birth of Christ - who was probably not born at that time of the year anyway. (The Gregorian calendar was only invented at a later date).

Jesus was resurrected at Easter. Once more the celebrations are mixed with the Fertility cult: the resurrection of the earth with its Easter eggs, bunny rabbits, newborn lambs and daffodils.

Harvest Festival is a Christian tradition when the produce of the land is brought to the altar in thanksgiving... Yet this is another Pagan practice although quite acceptable when cloaked in Christianity.

In the above I just wished to point out that Wicca, Paganism etc. are totally unrelated to Black Magic.

Strange, how we seem to have gone full circle and are back to natural food, herbal drinks and cures. Suddenly it has become important to plant trees and preserve the rain forests. We now acknowledge the wisdom of Native Americans. Missionaries have done much damage in their religious zeal by imposing their own, often impractical values on people who lived close to nature.

All over the world tribes have independently practised similar rituals for centuries. When important decisions have to be made for the benefit of the tribe the witch doctor will go into a trance with the help of the same hallucinogenic plants his ancestors used for the purpose. This enables him to ask the advice of his forefathers or of his animal spirit guide. (In the Amazon the Jaguar is a favourite). The drug is used for this specific reason only, unlike many of today's young people who will take anything haphazardly to "go on a trip" - damaging both their brain and their health in the process.

Black Magic, Sorcery, Voodoo and Curses

Do you believe in Black Magic (not the chocs), demons and curses, or do you think they are just a load of mumbo-jumbo for illiterate people? Are you of the opinion that characters who stick pins in dolls only exist in late night horror movies - not to be taken seriously - or does the whole subject make you feel rather uneasy? Let me assure you that sorcery IS a fact and DOES work. On the whole it is scorned upon by educated people and by the Church. However, it is practised all over the world.

African clients look upon me as a Western witch doctor. They treat me with great respect and awe - which I found quite amusing at first. They ask me for amulets to ward off the evil eye or to cure various complaints:

- "My mother-in-law doesn't like me. Could you give me some powder to sprinkle around my bed?" - or else:

- "Would you advise me to put garlic cloves between my toes as protection against sorcery?"

As soon as they are ill they suspect someone of putting a curse on them. How many times have I reassured them:

 - "You are aching all over? It's probably arthritis, due to the damp climate - no, it's definitely not Ju-Ju. Try codliver oil or garlic tablets... and how about asking your doctor's advice?"

Mixing up magic potions to please them is something I am not prepared to do. In their vulnerability I could easily have sold them ordinary sea-shells as amulets at an exorbitant price. (This reminds me of my mother who brought back from holidays a souvenir containing "genuine earth from the Holy Land" when she could have picked it for free.)

As a rule I always go out of my way to help people for a very modest fee and often free of charge. A man offered me tiny plastic eyes and elephants at 5p each - with a 5% discount if I bought a whole bagful. He assured me:

- "It is good business. Sell them to your clients at £5 each or more as protective amulets. Tell them it will bring them good luck."

He would not take no for an answer and in the end I slammed the phone down in disgust.

When people come to me because they feel someone is sending them negative thoughts, nine times out of ten their fears are unfounded:

 - "Nothing is going right in my life at the moment. I must be cursed."

What nonsense! There is not a single person on this earth who sails through life without worries.

Sue, a West-Indian teenager, was sent to me by her family because she had become unbearably moody and irritable. They believed that a curse was preventing her from finding suitable employment.

First of all, Sue's parents had taken her to see an Obiah - a "Woman of God" - to remove the evil influence. The lady had given Sue a ritual bath with herbs while chanting a spell and slitting a live chicken's neck on the girl's head, spilling the blood all over her. (Not a very pleasant but apparently common practice in the West Indies).

- "And did you find a job afterwards?" I enquired politely.

- "No", she sighed. "That is why I have been sent here now."
(Oh, dear! Why me?)

My sitter seemed moody indeed - she was no ray of sunshine... maybe because she resented visiting me. However, she accepted healing which calmed her down. I really could not feel anything psychically wrong. Maybe she suffered with P.M.T.

So I suggested a visit to the doctor's, adding: "You can't find a job because of the current recession and because you have no qualifications. Why don't you go to college and study something useful? There is no shortcut to studies and hard work. And... try smiling for a change!"

That simple solution seemed to solve the problem and she left in a much happier frame of mind.

But Nigerian Joe really took the biscuit:

- "Muriel, I have a problem with a woman. Can you help? She is pregnant and refuses to have an abortion. What is your advice?"

- "Well, you don't have to marry her if you don't want to, but it's her body and she is free to go ahead and have the baby if she so wishes. You should at least help her financially to support the child."

- "She is a BAD woman! She is breaking up my marriage."

- "If you have such a good partnership already then why are you sleeping with another woman? It takes two to tango."

- "My mistake! This is where you come in. I want you to abort the child at a distance by psychic methods."

- "Sorry, I wouldn't do that: it would be wrong and evil."

Furious he yelled:

- "Then you are no good as a medium!" and slammed the phone down.

People from all over the world were telling me strange unpalatable stories. A South American lady confided:

- "My sister has just died in mysterious circumstances. She was only 19 and in good health. Yet within a week she was dead. It's sorcery, you see. Everyone in my family is afraid, wondering who is going to be next. Maria was used as a sacrifice in a satanic ritual. Six months ago my father died suddenly. Then my brother. Now I am too scared to go home." (Who can blame her?)

Even here in London I was informed by a panic stricken woman:

- "My friend who is 16 is very ill in hospital. The consultants can't find the cause of her complaint. But we all know it's sorcery so would you please go and remove the curse? I shall pay your taxi fares." (That's generous!)

At the time, being a mere novice, I declined politely, having no wish to fight a sorcerer.

A fortnight later the same woman called:

- "My friend has just died. Thought you'd like to know. You could have saved her..."

She had more faith in me than I had. Besides at the time I didn't have a clue how to combat Black Magic.

A Ghanaian lady is struggling alone in London to bring up her small child. She has applied to emigrate to Canada - the further from home the better:

- "I am terrified to go back in case someone casts a spell on my daughter - like 'they' did on the rest of the family who died at various intervals of unknown causes.

It seems that when one person is prosperous another is jealous and immediately consults a witch doctor who sends a curse to the family - who in turn retaliate by going to his competitor in the business.

A Pakistani lady assured me that her little brother had been possessed by a demon. He would go out at night when there was a full moon and howl like an animal. The poor boy was dutifully exorcised by prayers and 'beating the devil out of him'.

A Polynesian sitter who wished to open a restaurant on his island offered to pay my fare there:

- "Just pack your bags and come along. As a medium you will be in great demand. You will have no trouble setting yourself up in business."

Puzzled, I wondered: why this sudden generosity from a perfect stranger? He soon put me in the picture:

- "The witch doctor has cursed me and I am scared. He warned me never to return or else... Now with your protection I would have nothing to fear, would I? And we could both become prosperous too".

My Thoughts on the Subject

Sifting through dozens of similar cases I wondered: Is any of this possible? Reluctantly, I have come to the conclusion that a lot of it is - although often mixed with superstition and ignorance.

The sorcerer exerts an enormous amount of power, being both feared and respected. Over the years I have met a number of people who dabble in Black Magic but I have never fraternised with witch doctors or sorcerers. Some of them are probably highly intelligent individuals capable of performing excellent cures while others are dangerous characters - or maybe they are a mixture of both.

I leave you to make up your own mind. But I do know for a fact that when a person knows that he is cursed he often gives up and literally dies of fear.

Protecting Yourself

As a rule a curse won't touch you if you reject it. Poison can harm you physically but negative thoughts will bounce off when you are spiritually and mentally strong, that is why they are often directed to the weakest member of a family, such as a child.

All you have to do really is ask that the curse be returned to its sender. You then say a prayer asking for protection while imagining yourself being slowly immersed in a tranquil pond and then rising out of the water closing down your main chakras - or psychic centres - like seven bolts. These are:

1. The top of the head
2. The Clairvoyant Eye (the space between the eyebrows)
3. The throat
4. The heart
5. The Solar Plexus
6. The spleen
7. The lower part of the spine.

Mentally wrap yourself up in a cloak of light. If God is represented by a Light and you surround yourself with His love nothing can touch you. You can do the same for your children. This exercise DOES work but you have to concentrate. However, it is only basic information. There are many excellent books on psychic self-defence.

The average person has nothing to fear from Black Magic unless they are already involved in it or have an enemy who is. If you feel that wearing a religious symbol around your neck will protect you, then it will. It's all the power of thought - one of the most potent forces in the world. Although the article is only a piece of metal it represents the power of God and lower entities will stay away from it.

Cases of Possession

Occasionally I do feel a dark shadow around a sitter, but very seldom. Besides, I would not normally say anything unless they ask for help. I'd just recommend that they have spiritual healing and stay off hallucinogenic drugs. A person who is under the influence of dark forces knows so, having already experienced strange, eerie occurrences around them.

On the other hand I have recognised genuine cases of possession. It happened as recently as last week. The minute my visitor sat down at the table opposite me and looked into my eyes I felt shivers going down my spine. Although she was friendly and relaxed I was quite uneasy. (Oh, why had I let her in!) Suddenly, she leaned forward and smiled and for a split second her personality changed into something malevolent, her dark eyes suddenly bright and staring while she scrutinized me menacingly. The atmosphere in the room had turned cold too, charged with negative energy.

The whole incident only lasted a few minutes but I had sufficient time to see the face of an old hag overshadowing hers. Afterwards, the sitting carried on as normal, my client totally unaware of my misgivings. Now at this stage why, you may ask, did I not tell her that she was possessed? Because it is none of my business. She never mentioned the subject and I was certainly not going to either. Maybe she was happy with her situation as it was and I had no wish to interfere. Besides, fighting an evil entity is no fun. So remaining very pleasant I got rid of her as fast as possible. Just as she left, the other inhabitant of her body came through and glared at me for a second. Sighing with relief, I shut the door behind them both.

People may become possessed from drug abuse, sorcery or dabbling with the occult and getting their wires crossed. All these practices attract spirits, some good and others not so amiable. My advice is: don't play about with unknown forces.

Once I saw a a sitter leave with a small dark shadow trotting along behind him. Occasionally, the entity detaches itself and, choosing to remain with me, settles down defiantly in my front room. After saying goodbye to my sitter at the door I return to the lounge and discover that my home has suddenly become strangely hostile. Shivering I stand still and glance around slowly...

Oh, dear! The draught is coming from the left corner, near the window... There it is!... a dark presence leering at me threateningly. (Now at this stage most people would panic).

Politely I ask: - "Excuse me, but would you mind leaving? This is my home!"

The evil spirit takes no notice whatsoever and is now coming towards me, sneering maliciously. In some cases he is surrounded with pulsating electricity, similar to lightning.

Unperturbed I stand my ground:

- "Sorry, you'd better leave, you can't touch me anyway. I am on God's side... Let me show you the light!" and, taking a step forward, I imagine that my hands are full of rays of sunshine which I now hurl at him. (The spirit can actually see the light projected by my mind and recoils).

After a while he will disintegrate in front of my eyes - just like a character in a science fiction film. If he is still resilient and refuses to leave I open the window wide and, pointing to the road outside, I yell:

- GET OUT ! Do you hear: O U T !!"

So far this method has proved successful. These occurrences, however, are few and far in between. It's just a question of standing up to the entity and showing that you are in charge. Of course, I owe my aplomb to the presence of my spirit helpers. Once the atmosphere has been cleared the room reverts to its usual peaceful atmosphere.

There are a few easy methods for clearing a place. The traditional Roman Catholic tradition of blessing the four corners of the room with holy water is efficient, or a simple Banishing ritual works too. If in doubt, seek professional help.

The first time someone possessed came to me for help I was at a loss, not knowing how to help her. On the telephone she had simply requested a reading but when this plump and shy middle aged woman arrived she suddenly blurted out:

- "I am possessed. Can you help me?"

Shocked, I gasped: "Er... I... I beg your pardon?"

(Help! What do I do now?) Perhaps the most sensible thing would be to try and call the experts. My sitter waited patiently, confident that I would help her, while I feverishly telephoned several vicars, priests and established exorcists - but no one was available. Although reluctant to tackle the matter myself I soon realised that this was exactly what my spirit friends expected me to do. A message kept flashing through my mind: "Oh, ye of little faith!"

Meanwhile my patient sat quietly flicking through the pages of a magazine. You'd think she was in the dentist's waiting-room. In the end, I offered her healing which she gratefully accepted. It was only then that I realised just how powerful guides can be. Feeling myself growing taller and taller as the Native

147

American took over, I was shown exactly how to clear the person's aura and banish the entity. When my hands touched the nape of the patient's neck something solid knocked me back and brushed past in a hurry leaving a nasty smell of rotten eggs in its wake.

The woman jerked me back to reality as she exclaimed joyfully:

- "It's gone! The entity has just left. What a relief!"

And, indeed, the atmosphere in the room had lifted. Looking up in a daze I noticed golden rays of sunshine gently filtering in through the window. I felt exhilarated: the entity had been banished, the room felt lovely and warm.

Since my first attempts at exorcism I have dealt with other cases quite successfully. Spirit never gives more than you can cope with and they are always there to give a helping hand.

Psychiatrists would do well to study the subject of possession in more depth because some patients truly do hear voices or see spirits, in which case the services of a medium would be of great help. If, say, a pianist maintains that he (or she) is inspired by Beethoven, it's quite possible. After all, why shouldn't the composer wish to link in with a sensitive who would play his new compositions? But if a person makes an exaggerated statement, for example, that Jesus has ordered him to take on the world's sins on his own shoulders, thereby saving the universe... or something else on those lines, it's obvious that he needs help.

As a rule, I don't offer to clear a patient of an entity nor a house of a ghost. They approach me. It's only when I am quite sure that they are not imagining things that I agree to help. First of all I speak kindly to the spirit, explaining that he should leave. It is usually sufficient. I never frighten anyone, always remaining calm and reassuring. In my work I am sincere, acting as a transmitter for my guides to come through and help the sitter. Their presence makes me feel totally confident. It took many years of training before we achieved this close synchronisation.

There are ruthless charlatans around who frighten people by telling them that they are cursed or possessed when they are not. They charge exorbitant prices to remove these imaginary evils. Should this happen to you, refuse to pay and seek a second and third opinion. Do not be afraid to report them to the police. You will do genuine mediums and exorcists a favour. Above all, use your own judgment. If a reading does not make sense, reject it in no uncertain terms..

Now, in contrast young Tracy was someone I won't forget in a hurry: Black Magic was a thrilling subject she found irresistible. Far from being afraid she expected me to... teach her the Dark Arts! Her outfit advertised her ambitions in life for, like a character in a cartoon, she wore a long black skirt, a tee-shirt with skulls, black lipstick and nail varnish to match. Her silver earrings and bracelets were resplendent with tibias, bats, upside-down crosses and pentagrams.

Flicking back her long dark mane she looked around, totally disappointed at the ordinary surroundings.

We sat down and I started to give her a reading. However, Tracy was not paying attention. After some hesitation she came to the real purpose of her visit".

- "Could you arrange for me to act with Vincent Price in his next Dracula film? And, by the way, do you run a Black coven and may I join? Can you teach me how to put curses on people and call up Satan? My lucky number is 666... I am interested in... EVIL - it's... SO EXCITING!" (And indeed, she was shaking with the thrill of it all).

I soon put her right!

The best one was a request I overheard in a psychic bookshop. An odd looking character in a grey raincoat with upturned collar was whispering under his breath:

- "Do you have a Book of Curses... not only for the Living but... for the DEAD?...."

The salesman's face was a picture as he looked up, open mouthed, his gold rimmed glasses slipping to the tip of his nose.

Giggling uncontrollably I heard him muttering: "Well, hmmm... hmmm..."

Mediumship has its funny side! Having watched too many late night films some of my visitors shiver with fear as they enter my home, expecting a set from the "Amityville Horror" film. They think I sleep in a coffin and that spectres sail across the room. When they have to answer the call of nature they cross their legs even tighter until at last in desperation they whisper:

- "Do you have a bathroom?"

- "Straight up the winding stairs to the turret. But watch out for the ghost of the Lady in Grey. She was there first."

One memorable Sunday evening the bathroom door came off its hinges. Upon inspection I discovered that both fittings were broken. Now the loose door stood leaning against the wall. As a client had made an appointment for the following morning and all the shops were closed we decided that she could not possibly use a loo without a door. So my son came to the rescue. He removed the hinges from the airing cupboard and fitted them onto the bathroom door so that at least it would shut. As there were no spare hinges Nathan simply stood the other door up against the airing cupboard.

Now the following day a very nervous young lady arrived, shaking with nerves. In an attempt to make her relax I smiled:

 - "Do sit down at the table. Would you like a cup of tea or coffee?"

Soon she was clutching her mug while looking around fearfully. In vain I tried to alleviate her fears and make her feel comfortable:

- "It's not as bad as the dentist's! Would you like a biscuit? A sandwich?"

She declined my offer. So I spread out the Tarot cards, the silence broken by the sound of her chattering teeth. Why did she want a reading if she was so afraid? What on earth did she think was going to happen?

Then suddenly the quietness was shattered by a loud

C-R-A-S-H !!

in the hall as the airing cupboard door fell with a terrific noise across the hall onto the central heating. (My sitter must have brushed against it when she came in.)

The poor girl screamed: "AAAGGHHH!" and scrambled to her feet rushing to the front door while I collapsed with laughter. It was too funny for words. Running behind her I caught her arm and showed her the ghost from beyond: a door without hinges!

Finally she calmed down, started to laugh too and from then on enjoyed her reading.

The Strange Case of Sam Katz

The phone was ringing persistently in the hall.

Oh, no! It was still night time... 5.30 a.m. Why can't I just ignore the noise and carry on sleeping?

Groggily I pulled on my dressing gown and, yawning, went into the passage:

- "Hello, can I help you?...." (If it was an obscene phone call I'd give him a piece of my mind, that's for sure....)

There was a silence at the other end...

- "Yes? HELLO!"... (Now what?)

A faint male voice was whispering: "Help m e...."

Oh, dear! Forcing myself to wake up in a hurry I encouraged him gently:

- "What is your name? Come on, friend, talk to me."

The croaky voice gasped: "Sam..."

- "Yes, Sam. Do you have tonsillitis?"

- "No... I am so depressed... H e l p m e. The rope is hanging in front of me... it's ready..."

- "Oh, for Heaven's sake, things can't be that bad surely..."

After another prolonged silence I called softly:

- "Sam, are you still there?"

- "I am going to finish it all... put an end to this misery..." he muttered.

- "Surely while there is life there is hope. Would you like to talk about it?"

One minute I was fast asleep and the next I was trying to talk this stranger out of taking his own life. My heart was pounding... my mind still not fully alert. This man was genuinely suicidal. If I did not choose my words carefully he could easily be pushed over the brim. Then he started to talk, very slowly at first, one painful word at a time, as he tried to concentrate. (This was going to take all night. How on earth was I going to get up in the morning? Oh, well, never mind. If it helped then it was worth it.) As the phone had a long lead I ventured into the kitchen and put the kettle on.

- "I am Sam Katz. My ancestors were Jewish immigrants from Eastern Europe... Anyhow, to cut a long story short, at the end of the war I was a young soldier, about nineteen. At the time, war criminals were put on trial... made a lot of publicity in the papers, do you remember?"

- "The trial of Nuremberg?"

- "Well, no, not that one, but something similar on a smaller scale. During the course of the prosecution I was put in charge of guarding the cell of one of the condemned prisoners. All night, I stood there, my rifle on my shoulder, pacing up and down. At some point, out of curiosity, I suppose, I peered at the woman in the cell. Our eyes met... she stared at me... and..." (here his voice faltered) "it was such a shock... she was only my age, even younger maybe - a lovely young person. There and then, I fell in love with her, helplessly wishing I could do something to save her life. We kept looking at each other... but never said a word. I couldn't speak German... just knew her name was Ursula."

(By now his voice was barely audible... the memory too painful):

- "The next morning at 6 o'clock, they came to fetch her... and the others... It was horrible. I watched the officer putting a noose around her neck... that poor, sweet girl. Then she was jerked up in the air... swinging ... right in front of me... and the others were hanged next to her... Oh. God, I felt sick...

Her ghost has haunted me all these years... I love her, you understand... didn't want her to die... It's my duty to help her, protect her... Must go to her now. It's the only solution..."

Trying to take all this in at once in the middle of the night with my head in a spin, I first took a sip of hot coffee before answering:

- "Just a minute... The war was over ages ago. So why commit suicide at this stage?"

- "You don't understand. She is here with me, talks to me, tells me to come to her. We want to be together at last..."

152

- "And you actually believe her? Don't be ridiculous! She hates Jews - just wants you to die so that there is one less of your race on the earth. Tell me: why do you think Ursula was hanged? Because she was exerting her authority in a death camp. Young as she was, she probably enjoyed her power over helpless people, parading with Alsatian dogs, encouraging them to assault starving women and children. Come to your senses, Sam! That woman doesn't love you! She despises you, HATES you!"

- "Don't say that... It hurts..."

- "But it's the truth! You must get rid of her. She is evil."

(Accusing and condemning a woman I did not even know is not my usual practice - but on the spur of the moment, it was the only way I could think of stopping this man from committing suicide. Yet, subconsciously - was it telepathy? I knew I wasn't far wrong.)

- "Muriel, the urge to hang myself is getting stronger... I can't resist anymore."

- "Listen, Think of the shock your death would cause your family and friends. Is it fair on them? You are ALIVE! Ursula is dead... Anyone who could walk around Belsen or Dachau and remain indifferent to human suffering on such a scale is not worth much in my books... Just imagine, if it had been YOUR relatives in the camp..."

- "MMMmm... You've got a point, I suppose."

- "Instead of hanging yourself, just phone me - anytime. It doesn't matter. I'll do my best to talk you out of it."

He finally rang off. It was 7.30... two hours later. Exhausted, I was much too tense to even think of going back to bed.

And so over the following weeks Sam phoned at 5.30 - nearly every morning. It was a battle of wills:

- "I have just phoned to say good-bye, Muriel. It's the best thing. I want to be with Ursula. The rope is ready."

- "You are NOT, do you hear... NOT going to hang, I won't let you.

Afterwards during the day I was tired and irritable, walking around like a Zombie. Still, if it kept the poor bloke alive...

Sam had done well for himself. He was a chartered accountant and lived in St John's Wood, a select area of London. He also confided that he was single and, for some unknown reason, had never been able to keep a relationship for long. (Maybe that was why he had these fantasies about Ursula.) Yet, he sounded sane and, when not too depressed, quite a pleasant man.

The phone calls left me shattered, my usual vitality gone. His depression was starting to rub off on me. Uneasily, I realised that I was not alone at home anymore: something sinister was lurking around... I could feel its presence - my cosy, cheerful flat was slowly turning cold... full of dark shadows...

On that particular morning, I'd just put the phone down after another stressful discussion when, sighing with exhaustion, I turned around and... came face to face with Ursula's ghost standing defiantly in front of the cooker! Startled, I took a good look nonetheless at this misty appearance, the object of Sam's affections: here was a slim young blonde, her hair pulled back in a roll around her head. She wore a straight grey skirt with a white short-sleeved shirt and black laced up shoes.

My first impulse was to snap at her in German: - "Why don't you leave Sam alone and let me go back to bed, you stupid cow. You are wasting everybody's time!"

But good manners prevailed. However - oh, dear! - she'd picked my thoughts... The look that those steely blue eyes gave me was one of pure hatred.

- "You don't frighten me, Ursula! Just go away, I am not one of your prisoners".

(At this stage it may be helpful for me to explain once more that if I project an image in my mind a spirit can see it.)

So, concentrating, I visualised white light pouring down on the Nazi. It worked... for she recoiled, a look of fear on her face. She took a step back... straight through the cooker... and disappeared altogether.

(Phew! That was a close one...)

So now I knew why I was feeling so washed out. It was not only due to lack of sleep. Discussing the woman had attracted her earthbound spirit to my flat. In my weakened state she had managed to get through my defences, helping herself to my energy with which she was able to manifest. God knows what other sinister characters had also arrived to invade my privacy.

Somehow, I knew this was only the beginning...

With foreboding I waited, alone in the gathering dusk...

I had stood up to Ursula, chased her fearlessly from my home and now she was scheming a new attack!

Maybe it was time to ask for help. Wearily I called a couple of healer friends of mine:

- "Helen, could you and Tony give me a hand? I need some extra power tonight to fight a psychic attack"... and I explained the circumstances, glad to hear my friend's reassuring voice:

- "Of course, Muriel, anytime. This evening at 8 p.m. our group will hold a Rescue Circle. Hopefully, we might be able to contact Ursula and send her off to the Light."

At about 10 p.m. Helen rang:

- "Seven of us gathered in my front room. You will be glad to know that we managed to get through to her. The place grew very cold and suddenly Ursula appeared in the middle of our circle. We explained that she must go to the Next World and leave Sam alone. She sneered in derision... Ugh! The sound of that high-pitched laughter still makes me shudder... You were right when you mentioned the Powers of Darkness! We are definitely linking in with evil forces... And I have a hunch that there's more to it than Ursula. She is just a pawn for something much bigger. It's not over yet.... Be careful, Muriel. And - by the way" (here her tone became cheerful again): "we are very happy to be of service".

Dear, kind Helen. It was good to know I had extra power to fight whatever still lay ahead. Feeling much calmer I went to bed and slept peacefully. Unbeknown to me malevolent presences were silently invading my bedroom...

In the middle a of the night I tossed around in bed... What was that loud thumping noise? Was it the sound of my heartbeats?... My subconscious mind was urging: - "Come on Muriel, hurry! W A K E U P!"

Startled I sat up bold straight in bed and stared around in the darkness.

Something was moving....

I didn't like the sound of it at all...

Cold and shivering I reached out for my bed jacket and wrapped it around my shoulders.

Looking up towards the window I was confronted by a menacing shadow looming at the foot of my bed... and recognised Ursula! Still in her short-sleeved blouse and skirt she just stood there, motionless... peering at me intently, a triumphant sneer on her face. Her thoughts rang, loud and clear, in my mind:

- "I haven't finished with you yet! You can't get the better of me!"

While I lay asleep she had again managed to take my energy in order to build her own ghostly presence.

Turning her head around, Ursula held up her hand, signalling to someone behind her...

It was as though she had opened a door to let in a hurricane, for great gusts of freezing cold wind came blowing across my room, their sheer force throwing me back against the wall.

In the darkness I sat up alone facing the forces of Evil, gasping for air, choking.... my heart beating violently at an increasing pace. Was I having a heart attack? Something else was building up in the night... and it was taking what little power I had left in order to do so. Clutching my chest, I thought I was going to pass out or die altogether.

The thumping noise was growing louder... I recognised it now - it was the sound of soldiers marching towards me... their boots treading rhythmically as they advanced...

What lay ahead?

Transfixed, I waited... linking in with the prisoners' terror all those years ago... as, helplessly, they had watched the Gestapo approaching... Within a matter of seconds, their fate would have been sealed, while the guards decided, at the flick of a finger, who would live and who would die. The suspense was dreadful.

156

Suddenly a platoon of ghostly Nazis in their grey uniforms were entering my bedroom through the wall, bolts of lightning hissing around them...

THEY WERE COMING STRAIGHT AT ME!

The leader in front commanded telepathically, pointing towards my bed:

- "SEIZE HER!"

I screamed back at him:

- "Oh, no you don't! I am with God, with the Light. You can't touch me!" and started to pray, desperately asking my guides to come to my rescue.

But still they were advancing...

Drawing pentagrams in the air, I did a quick Banishing Ritual. At that moment the lightning bolts increased, flashing all around the room.

NO! Come what may, I was determined to fight!

And the next minute... both Ursula and the soldiers shrivelled up in front of me, like burnt out bits of paper...It was all over. The battle had been won. Exhausted but happy I got out of bed and switched on the light: my home was slowly regaining its peaceful atmosphere. The room felt warm again.

That morning, at 5.30, Sam phoned again. Still half asleep, I whispered:

- "You're okay now. Ursula has gone and won't trouble you anymore. By the way, did she have blue eyes, blonde hair pulled back in a roll around her head and was she wearing a straight grey skirt and a short-sleeved blouse?"

Sam whistled softly, taken aback, before answering: - "Well, I never... Yes... yes indeed, that was her alright... It's amazing. But tell me: what happened?"

So I gave him an account of the night's events. He felt shocked at what I had been through but doubtful as to whether the woman really had left.

But that same afternoon he called again, cheerful for the first time:

- "I can't believe it... but it's true: a great weight which I have been carrying around for years, has suddenly lifted. I feel like a new man".

- "Now you must get Ursula out of your mind and not call her back and everything will be fine. I also know now why all your girlfriends dropped you after a short while: because Ursula's ghost overshadowed them in bed..."

He thought my remarks over for a while before answering:

- "How incredible! Yes, it all fits in now... Caroline running off in the middle of the night without an explanation... just when I thought we were getting on so well."

The following day, at lunchtime, Sam announced:

- "Guess what. I contacted Caroline this morning and we had a long talk. It was difficult trying to explain to her how Ursula had possessed me all those years... But the amazing thing is that she knew already... you were right... Ursula had tried to take her over too!

The first and only time we slept together Caroline had suddenly become rigid with fear as she'd felt another cold, suffocating presence inside the bed trying to take her body over. Apparently I had stared at her unseeingly, calling her 'Ursula' (can't remember ever doing that) and, wrapping my arms around her neck, told her that she would hang. Terrified, Caroline had jumped out of bed, gathered her clothes in a hurry and rushed off into the night. Later on, when I had tried to talk to her on the telephone she had slammed the receiver down. Poor girl! No wonder...

But now Caroline has decided to give me another chance... if I am sure Ursula has gone for good." After a pause he added: "She is such a kind, understanding person. I am very lucky..."

Then unexpectedly he asked: "May I come and see you? I wish to thank you personally for your help."

After some hesitation I agreed. Two days later Sam turned up on my doorstep. What sort of a man would Sam be? A sleek black BMW was pulling up in front of my home. Minutes later the doorbell rang and I had my first glimpse of a well dressed man in a dark suit and expensive silk tie. He had thick curly white hair.

- "Do come in, Sam!" I welcomed him.

He smiled as he entered, kissed me on the cheek, said: "Hello" to the boys and sat down on the settee. Over the next half hour, my visitor sipped a cup of herbal tea, chatting amiably about banalities. He was a pleasant, gentle character - the image of middle-class respectability. His green eyes, behind thick glasses, had a look of sadness.

Conversation proved difficult and I was running out of inspiration. Finally, he finished his tea and rose to leave. At the door, he smiled again and, squeezing my hand, whispered: "Thanks for everything". Then he was gone.

Sam never phoned again. I hope he followed my advice and put the past behind, starting a new life with Caroline... But somehow, I wonder whether he did... His girlfriend was probably a nice, reliable and predictable person whereas Ursula provided the element of danger and excitement in his otherwise humdrum life.

The ball was in his court. What happened in the end I shall never know...

Many more, even stranger experiences were to follow...

Chapter Eleven

Loneliness

Loneliness is one of the problems of modern society. In days gone by, when people lived in villages, everyone knew each other. Perhaps they gossiped and got on each other's nerves but at least there was a spirit of togetherness. The back door was kept unlocked. (Just imagine doing this today in London). When Grannie became old and frail she sat near the fire while the rest of the family looked after her.

Nowadays the old lady can go into a home and often the only caring visitors she sees are at her funeral. (Of course, there are still many people who do look after their elderly dependents). It's also awkward when relatives are in full-time occupation and the pensioner requires constant care. And, let's face it, Gran may be senile and impossible to live with. It's sad, though, that someone may be found dead in their own home after several weeks - or even months.

Young people imagine that marriage will solve all their problems, bringing eternal happiness. In fact many couples only remain together for the sake of their possessions. After years of bringing up a family, they have nothing left to say to each other once the children have left.

Retirement may also be a cause for friction. Supposing the husband had no other interests outside work he will suddenly feel useless. The wife had the freedom of the house for years and now her husband is at home all day getting on her nerves.

One partner often dominates the other who has lost his/her individuality. Old John was a perfect example. He'd sit for hours giving me a quick recap of his wartime experiences (which I'd already heard a dozen times) while his wife Jess, endlessly knitting away, would nod her head: "Yes... yes, that's right..." She even repeated his words like a parrot. They had become like two sides of the same coin.

When one of them dies the other forgets all the years of resentment, only remembering the good moments: "We were SO happy together... never argued." My parents, on the other hand, certainly retained their individuality! Dad loved telling old stories which he embellished over the years. Mum, however, would insist upon accuracy. When he happily launched himself:

- "It happened in France..." she would immediately intervene:

- "No, dear. It happened in Austria. Don't you remember? You had the blue Ford at the time."

But he would persevere:

- "Auntie Louise was with us on holidays."

To which Mum would snap:

- "Not that year. Really, dear, your memory...."

Irritated, Dad would shrug his shoulders:

- "Well, why don't you tell the story then?"

My father also loved repeating the same vintage jokes of which he had a whole repertoire. As soon as he enthusiastically said the first few words we knew exactly which yarn we would have to suffer for the next ten minutes.

Once, Mum asked him sweetly:

- "Why don't you number your jokes, Frank? Then all you will have to do is call out 'No 43!' and we'll all roar and save you the bother."

... Now that Dad has died Mum would give anything to hear him telling his familiar stale jokes again.

Christmas can be one of the loneliest times of the year. From October onwards commercials show people having a wonderful time celebrating with family and friends.

A person who is busy the whole year round will suddenly feel lonely and left out:

- "All these festivities... parties... and fun! Why doesn't anyone invite me?"

In December I could fill my home with sad people. The phone keeps ringing with depressed or suicidal individuals of all ages crying down the line. So, one

Christmas, I organised a get-together for lonely elderly neighbours. It was surprising just how many able-bodied pensioners declined my invitation although they had nothing else to do:

- "No. Don't think so... Thanks for asking anyway."

The party didn't cost much: I baked a large cake and mince pies, made a few sandwiches, put some crisps on a plate and bought a few inexpensive bottles. The front room was decorated with garlands and a Christmas tree. Just as I was putting on a record of Mrs Mills' playing old party tunes at the piano the first pensioners came trooping in. At first, they sat down, feeling shy and reserved, but after a while they started to unwind, chatting together like long lost friends.

Towards the end of the evening I suggested:

- "Now that you've all been officially introduced why don't you have a cup of coffee together from time to time or perhaps one of you could invite another person and take it in turns to cook a simple meal once a month?"

My neighbours all agreed it was a splendid idea, they'd had a great time and when would the next party be? Finally the last guests departed, arm in arm, singing merrily down the road. Most of these people have died since and not one of them ever invited another for a coffee and a chat. They were solitary and remained so until the end.

Loneliness hits most of us at times. Some senior citizens are so used to their own company that they can't cope with a visitor and refuse to attend a Day Centre. It's not always the neighbours' fault when a person is found dead after several days. At the time I had volunteered to visit elderly housebound people. Although most of the pensioners were very nice just the odd one or two were so unclean and aggressive that in the end no one dared ring their bell. At their funeral the priest conducted the service alone, reading out his own text and the absent congregation's reply in turn. A few days later, the deceased's meagre possessions were auctioned off to pay for the funeral costs.

So many individuals go through their solitary lives with no love to give and none to receive. They live in the past, feel miserable and are full of self-pity. If I enquire:

- "How are you today?" they reply:

- "To tell you the truth, I feel quite depressed. My arthritis is playing me up. My back aches. No one cares these days. It's also loneliness, I suppose... nothing to look forward to anymore."

- "Well, I know a nice lady who lives down the road. Would you like to meet her? Maybe I could bring her along sometime."

- "Oh, no dearie. I mind my own business. Yes, I'll talk to you but then I know you, it's different."

- "You didn't know me either a few months ago! How about joining the Community Centre? There is a range of activities for senior citizens: you can play cards, learn to draw or paint etc. - or you can just sit around and have a cup of tea and a natter. Or maybe you would like to go to the Day Centre? You'd meet other people, have a nice meal... If it's too difficult getting there on your own steam an ambulance could pick you up. I'd be pleased to make all the arrangements so you have nothing to worry about."

All of a sudden she panics and finds a dozen excuses: - "No, thanks all the same. I am very busy what with all the housework and my daughter who comes to see me once a month..."

This reminds me of an old lady who came to see me for a reading. She looked sad and lost as she sat on the edge of a chair clutching her handbag and staring vacantly into space. A little straw hat from a bygone era was perched on top of her straight grey hair.

Looking at the cards I ventured: "It seems your whole world has collapsed around you since he died."

She nodded in agreement, blinking back tears.

- "You feel his presence everywhere in the house... in fact, oh dear... you have even thought of taking your own life."

She nodded dejectedly: "Yes"... and blew her nose in her handkerchief before wiping the tears from her wrinkled face.

My heart went out to the poor widow. But, try as I could somehow I found it impossible to get through to her husband. Usually when a widow comes the spirit of her husband walks in behind her. This was strange... where was he?

Finally I asked: "Would you have something belonging to him? It would help... a photograph perhaps?"

To my astonishment my visitor burst into tears as she produced a dog's lead. Poor woman! The great love of her life was her poodle - the only being in the world who'd given her affection. No wonder I could not get through to her husband. She had never been married.

Eagerly, she leaned forward: "Tell me, what is he saying?"

What could I answer? "Woof! Woof?"

However, I managed to get the dog's name together with an accurate description of his temperament and habits. And why didn't she give another dog a good home? The old lady went home comforted in the knowledge that her pet would meet her in the next world.

Pets are great companions especially for people who live alone. It gives them a purpose in life: another being to cherish and care for. They don't feel lonely anymore and their daily routine revolves around the animal.

But some owners do go overboard! In particular I remember a person who once invited me for Sunday lunch. Much to my surprise she set out a tiny table with a white linen tablecloth for her cat and, fastening a bib around the poor creature's neck, insisted that he put his paws on the table and keep his hind legs on the floor while eating his food.

Another eccentric elderly woman I shall never forget used to walk down the High Street wearing a long Victorian dress and a frayed shawl. A large straw bonnet strewn with artificial flowers was tied with ribbons underneath her chin. To complete the picture she pushed an archaic pram and kept cooing at the baby inside. Upon closer inspection her infant turned out to be a Pekinese dog in a lace bonnet, neatly tucked in with a bib and a dummy around its neck.

While we are on the subject of animals, when people expect me to give their dog or cat a reading I draw the line. What am I supposed to say anyway?

- "Madam, your dog is sexually repressed and has tendencies towards neurosis. At present he lingers around lamp-posts in search of a sincere bitch of compatible astrological sign."

When I was younger I felt sorry for lonely people and still do. But I have now also learned to say 'No'.

Old May was a fine example of my gullibility. She was one of those hangers-on I collected over the years. Arriving unexpectedly she would make herself at home on the settee between my two boys, who were still very young at the time. Then she'd switch on the television to her favourite programme (ignoring the fact that both boys were eagerly waiting to see their cartoons). May never stopped talking - she was not a bundle of joy. Her comments never varied:

- "Awful weather today...Can't stand the flat I live in. My previous place was much better... Nobody speaks to me here...The price of bread is going up, I ask you! It's this government."

She would also order cups of tea and invite herself to lunch. (Now I would not have minded had she been of a more cheerful disposition). The boys couldn't stand the bitter old woman. We nicknamed her "Ye Merrie Month of May." While I was in the kitchen my eldest son would suggest:

- "Now why don't you go home and watch your own television, Grannie?"

- "Don't be so rude!... MURIEL! Your children are badly behaved! Now in my days WE had respect for our elders".

Four hours later May would sigh:

- "Well, I suppose I'd better go now."

The boys would both nudge each other, delighted at the good news.

Over the following ten minutes my uninvited guest would slowly put on her coat and felt hat, on top of which she'd spread a plastic rainhood, tying the bands under her chin.

As we all breathed a sigh of relief, she would glance around:

- "Well, I've changed my mind. This place is warm and besides, I have nothing else to do. Yes... I think I'll stop here for a bit longer."

Dismayed, we stared as she sat down again, unbuttoned her coat and reversed the whole process:

165

- "Now how about another cup of tea?"

Then and there I realised that charity begins at home. May was making our lives a misery. Still not able to stand up to her, the next (and last!) time she paid us a visit we kept very quiet, pretending there was no one in. But she would not leave and kept ringing the bell persistently, banging on the door and shouting through the letter-box:

- "Open the door! You can't fool me. I know you're in there. Let me in! Some folk have no manners..."

After a series of similar experiences I learned that it is much easier to stop an unpleasant situation immediately, rather than let it get out-of-hand. Whenever possible, I try to remain tactful and polite. An acquaintance of mine went even further. Barbara felt sorry for a tramp huddled up outside in the cold so she brought him in. The old man was very grateful. After a warm bath, he received clean clothes and sat down to a hearty meal. He spent a cosy night in the spare bedroom. The following morning after breakfast Barbara's guest thanked her profusely before disappearing down the road. Half an hour later she discovered that he had sneaked into her bedroom and stolen all her jewellery.

The whole world suffers with loneliness. Show me one single person who does not feel lonely at times! What is its cure?

1. Love! A great encompassing love for all that which is alive. The old adage "If you want to have a friend, be a friend" is as true today as it has always been.

2. Don't compare yourself to others who may seem to have all the luck while you are struggling along.

3. Live NOW. Don't look back. The worst thing you can do is sit down and start dwelling upon your fate.

4. If possible regular exercise - a sport or even spring cleaning - will give you a buzz.

5. Learn something new. You will meet people of like mind. There is no shortage of clubs and classes.

6. Make the most of your looks and your clothes - it will boost your confidence.

7. Be positive. Worries come and go. If you have a problem try and sort it out to the best of your ability then set it aside. Don't worry about what may - or may not - happen in the future. After all 90% of the fears you had, say five years ago, sorted themselves out alone - you don't worry about them now. Had you known all this at the time it would have saved a lot of stress. So the same applies with your worries today.

8. Decide what you are going to do with the rest of your life. Set yourself a goal - just out of reach - and go for it. It does not matter what your aim is but it should include using your intuition, your artistic talents and your emotions rather than the usual: "I want to be rich and famous." If you don't succeed today try again tomorrow or next week. Never be defeated. Don't allow your happiness to depend entirely upon a relationship or a career. Achieve something on your own so that at the end of your life you will be able to look back and say in sincerity: "I have left this earth a better place than when I arrived." Even if it's in a very small way you will have achieved something to be proud of.

Going Back in Time

Anne Boleyn is reputed to float down the main staircase at Hampton Court Palace. How many beheaded people silently glide across the Tower of London's courtyard at night?

Wouldn't it be interesting to visit an old manor house and be able to see the original owners and their staff walking around?

Well, this is possible when you learn to still your mind. It's very similar to psychometry, really, but instead of holding a piece of jewellery, you touch the wall or simply shut your eyes and link in with the atmosphere. Slowly the present recedes and you float back 100 years.... 500 years...

Whilst meditating in a historical place I start to see a faded picture reflected in the room... people in period costumes silently drifting by, a truly fascinating experiment, especially when at a later date their accuracy can be confirmed. The visions are not always pleasant either as past horrors somehow come back to life. Occasionally several generations drift in together - a strange historical replay.

It is also relatively easy to pin-point the exact spot where someone was murdered as opposed to the official place - or to locate the oldest part of a historical building. All you have to do, really, is pace up and down the area very slowly, feeling the psychic cold increasing as you near the spot, until at a specific place you stand still, shivering. Just imagine walking from warm sunshine into a cold cellar and back and you have the idea.

Have you ever visited the Temple Church in London? It is situated in a side street off The Strand. The building is circular in honour of the Holy Sepulchre Church in Jerusalem. The nave seems to have been annexed to it as an afterthought. Much has been written about these great Knights in shining armour - in fact, they are many young girls' dream image: Ah! to be swept away on a horse by a valiant warrior! It's a lovely, romantic notion but let's face it: those mighty warriors didn't wash very often, had no table manners and were proper male chauvinists - besides the fact that they had usually taken vows of chastity!

Tucked away in a corner, the church was not easy to find. On a warm, sunny day I ventured in through the porch and stepped into another world remote from the noisy road just around the corner. The nave stood ahead facing the altar to my right. Turning left I stepped into the circular building, empty but for stone statues of knights spread around on the floor. One even had his faithful dog at his feet. Everything was so peaceful with not a soul in sight except for the organist who was rehearsing Bach. The music seemed to waft up the pillars, rising in a sombre, powerful crescendo up to the vaults and beyond, linking the earth to an otherworldly dimension.

Enchanted, I sat down in a pew watching the sunshine filtering in through the stained glass windows. Soon I started to drift off... After a while the organist stopped playing and, tucking his music sheets away, he disappeared through a side door.

Still I carried on meditating, alone now in the church. Slowly a misty screen began to superimpose itself on top of the present decor. The chairs and pews had vanished and the floor was covered with straw. A large metal hoop with candles hung from the ceiling. The altar had also gone but another, more primitive version stood near the circular room. I was aware of whispering presences... ghostly knights trooping into the rotunda where they sat around in council. The lovely warm, spiritual atmosphere was replaced by an eerie feeling of impending doom... It hung in the air mingling with the smell of burning candles... Gradually the picture faded away and I returned to the 20th century. The sunshine was still pouring in through the windows... a golden ray dancing in front of me. I must have gone back in time and witnessed moments of terrible apprehension preceding a historical event. But which? All I know is that the Order was dissolved when the Knights, having become too prosperous, were accused of dreadful crimes...

168

In the silence I stretched my legs and walked to the stairs leading to the crypt... but couldn't bring myself to go down the steps. Something dark was lurking there... it made me feel uneasy. Perhaps someone had been murdered on that spot or else the warriors' ceremonies had not all been holy.

A month later I returned to the church with my son Nathan and a friend. We wandered around looking at the stone statues on the floor when the caretaker appeared. He was an amiable person and on an impulse I asked:

- "Could we possibly visit the gallery?"

The man seemed surprised:

- "Well... yes, why not? No one has ever expressed the wish to go up there... not much to see."

Obligingly, he selected a key from a large bunch and unlocked the door, allowing us to climb up a narrow winding staircase to the gallery. Halfway up, our host pointed to a small cell:

- "This is where a disobedient knight would be locked up and left to die. He could still look down and watch the ceremonies."

(How charming! Didn't I tell you there was a catch to these "perfect gentlemen"?)

As we climbed up the stairs the atmosphere became stiflingly silent, unspoilt by tourists' footsteps. The remote past was coming back to life. It would have been so much easier to link in here... Lost in thought I was jerked back to reality by the caretaker as he commented:

- "See those tiles... They were taken from the ground floor when the church was restored a while ago. And, by the way, we also discovered that the altar was not where it stands today... but over there!" and he pointed to the exact spot where I had seen it in meditation. That was just one of many similar experiences.

Do you know Glastonbury? It is one of the great psychic centres of England. Legend has it that when Joseph of Arimathea arrived in that area he planted his staff in the ground and it grew into a flowering tree which still stands there today. (Hmm... I am not convinced. What historical proof is there anyway that Joseph ever came to England in the first place? - Sorry, I am spoiling the story.)

169

Near the chapel, a tomb believed to contain the remains of King Arthur adds a romantic touch to the area and a little further down the road you will find a Celtic spring where the atmosphere is very peaceful. Glastonbury Hill is an old pagan site.

Anyhow, these are the main attractions apart from psychic book shops and various Tarot card readers offering their services. In my opinion - and for what it's worth - millions of tourists, trampling irreverently over the land, while eating beefburgers and chips, have wiped away some of its spiritual atmosphere. In order to rekindle the power dormant in these ancient sites one should tread quietly and respectfully as on a pilgrimage.

One of the eeriest and loveliest places I have ever visited is Glendalough, Co Wicklow, in Ireland. St Kevin was the founder of this ancient monastery, at present in ruins. It comprises the remains of a chapel, a round tower, an old graveyard - its Celtic crosses rising from the wild grass like spectres - a stream, woods and a lake surrounded with hills. The landscape is beautiful and when I arrived the sun was setting in gold and red hues over the cemetery. The psychic atmosphere was overpowering.

In the gathering dusk I became aware of a procession of chanting spirit monks filing by, each carrying a light in his hand. Tuning in, I 'saw' the monastery being ransacked - the shadow of a monk still hanging from the beams of a ruined cottage - while other prelates were scrambling up the tor.

On another occasion I returned to Glendalough on a grey morning. Clouds of mist were floating above the lake. In the stillness of this enchanting scenery I expected to see Merlin the Magician rising out of the vapour.

Various people have seen Roman soldiers marching in and out through their cellar wall. Others have picnicked in the countryside when suddenly they heard echoes of a fierce battle, fought centuries ago. This often occurs in Summer just before a storm. It's as if time stands still and you slot into a faded historical film.

The sceptic may comment: "Anyone can imagine pictures in time" - which is a fair comment.

If, for example, someone claims to have seen the ghost of Sir Walter Raleigh wandering around the Tower of London, the visitor may simply have had an overactive imagination. Although his encounter may have been genuine, the tourist was probably thinking of the great man as he entered the building. His brain was already conditioned to the possibility of meeting Sir Walter. So it

170

would have been easy enough to confuse imagination with reality. (Personally, I have never heard of ghosts appearing during the day to groups of noisy tourists).

On the other hand, let's take the example of someone driving down a lonely country lane when all of a sudden, out of the blue, a woman appears and throws herself under his car. The motorist stops his vehicle and leaps to the person's rescue... but no, there is no one to be seen either under the car or in the vicinity. He is in a state of shock believing he has killed her... Months later he learns that five years earlier, at that particular spot, a woman had indeed jumped to her death underneath a passing car. In that instance the driver had seen a picture re-enacted in time.

How to Cope With a Ghost

If you wake up one night to find a monk standing at the foot of your bed - and assuming that you don't hide under the sheets screaming your head off - you have three guesses as to the purpose of his presence:

1. You are clairvoyant and this is your spirit guide coming to say 'Hello';

2. The house was built on top - or in the vicinity of - an old monastery. This religious ghost is simply going about his daily business in the belief that he is still alive, or

3. You are seeing a picture in time, a traumatic event that happened centuries ago (maybe the monk was murdered on that spot) and now, under certain atmospheric conditions, you are watching an action replay. In this case the monk's spectre is just an empty shell who will probably be gliding above today's floor level (depending on its position in his days).

In any case don't worry about him. It's your bed - not his and you have every right to be there. Just say: "God bless you friend, what can I do for you?" You may get the answer in your mind. If you don't, just tell him: "Sorry, but please go away. This is my bedroom. You lived here ages ago." Don't forget that the poor spirit may probably be as scared as you are. He thinks YOU are a ghost haunting HIM. If he still refuses to move, add: "Let me show you the light" and then imagine a pathway of light going towards the sun. Saying a prayer at the same time will add strength to the procedure. The spirit will see this image and disappear. This method is usually sufficient to send ghosts off to the Next World.

If instead of a monk you recognise the ghost as being, say your Auntie Meg, do appreciate the effort she has made to come and see you. Don't scream: "Go away!". She is probably concerned about your well-being and just wishes you to know that she still cares and wishes to help. Just greet her: "Hello, Auntie Meg. Lovely to see you. What can I do for you?"

Talk to her and after a while, if she does not reply, just tell her kindly to leave. She will vanish immediately, for she comes with love, not to frighten you.

Perhaps you have moved to a house only to discover that it has a shady past... a woman jumped to her death from a bedroom window... Some of her despair remains impregnated in the walls. This person may still haunt the bedroom. Should you make her acquaintance, just send her off to the light as explained. The best antidote to depression in a house is laughter, gentle music, flowers, a fresh coat of paint and a light, cheerful colour scheme. Inviting a priest to come and bless the home is helpful but you can do it yourself by sprinkling Holy Water and visualising the room full of light.

Spirit Guides

Should you see a Native American, a Chinese mandarin, a Sister of-Mercy etc. these are usually spirit guides - or guardian angels - who protect you but normally you will only see them if you are already involved in spiritual work. They fill the atmosphere with peace - a totally different feeling to an encounter with the ghost of a restless soul.

Why are Indians, nuns and the like guardian angels? Because they were uncomplicated people who lived close to nature. They had none of the trappings of modern materialism so they are pure channels between this world and the next. For example, a nun does not come back to preach Roman Catholicism. She is beyond religious denominations and may simply be a female Being of Light whose habit matches her spiritual level. So the lady does not watch you in the bath nor is she interested in your bank balance. She just links in telepathically to inspire you when you use your intuition to either help others or to do something creative or artistic.

The Haunted Terraced House

The young woman's worried voice on the phone was pleasant and distinctly Irish:

- "Muriel, I hear you are a medium. Tell me now... do you perform exorcisms?"

- "Certainly, no problem!" (You'd think I do nothing else everyday, the way I was answering).

- "Would you be prepared to come to my house? We have just moved in and..." (Here, her voice faltered - she was obviously uneasy). "You won't laugh, will you but... the place is haunted."

- "Okay, don't worry. I believe you".

- "The presence of a tall man regularly follows me around the house. Often I catch a glimpse of him as he disappears through the wall. I KNOW I am not imagining things... To tell the truth: it's frightening".

- "Don't panic. He is probably just as scared of you as you are of him. Not realising that he has died he thinks YOU are the ghost haunting him. Of course, I shall come".

Kathleen was interested in my comments. She said she would contact me again to arrange an appointment. And sure enough, a few days later she phoned. This time her voice was more offhandish:

- "Muriel. It's me again, Kathleen. Remember? We won't require your services after all. Our priest is coming tonight to perform a blessing. HE knows all about these things and what to do. We are Roman Catholics and don't believe in mediums". (Thanks!)

- "Well, that sounds great. I am sure all prayers help. Thank you very much for letting me know and the best of luck tonight".

Three days later Kathleen was on the phone again. This time her voice was almost apologetic:

- "Hi, it's me again. The priest has been and blessed the house. He was very good... but the ghost is still there. Er... could you come? My husband now, he ridiculed the whole story but I tell you, last night he went to bed early, feeling tired. He was half asleep when he heard the sound of heavy footsteps coming into the room. Then a solid weight fell on top of him! Startled he jumped out of bed, switched on the light and looked around but... there was no one else to be seen yet he could still feel the presence a few yards away from him. The place felt freezing cold... Now he believes my story!"

- "The poor ghost's bed was probably at the same place and now he is thinking, just like one of the Three Bears: 'Who's been sleeping in my bed?'"

So this is how, the following week-end, with the A to Z in hand, I wound my way to a Victorian house in Streatham. Why did I expect a spooky old building? The place seemed so disappointingly ordinary. There was nothing to distinguish it from the other houses in the street. Mind you, they all looked grey on this cold, wet and miserable evening. I was missing a good programme on television into the bargain. My coat was drenched. With resignation I closed my dripping umbrella, walked up to the front door and rang the bell. (At least the setting was fine for a ghost story!)

The door opened almost immediately. An attractive blonde woman in a pale blue tracksuit greeted me with evident relief:

- "Ach, 't is good of you to come. Let me take your coat, you are soaking wet. Come and warm yourself in front of the fire while I put the kettle on." Although friendly and hospitable, Kathleen was also very nervous. Perhaps she was expecting someone in a black cloak. Smiling, I resisted the temptation to tell her that I had parked my broomstick outside.

We settled down to a cosy chat. After a while I suggested:

- "Tell you what, why don't you have another cup of tea while I look around for your ghost?"

My hostess was quite relieved at being let off the hook. As I went into the hall she called out: "The radiators are on full but you will still feel the cold at the top of the stairs."

She was right about the chilly feeling! Freshly painted white walls, boxes everywhere and a pile of clothes stacked in a corner confirmed that the couple had recently moved in. Slowly I walked down the hall and progressed upstairs trying to tune into the atmosphere. The cold grew more intense at the entrance to the main bedroom facing the stairs. Turning around I crept downstairs again towards the front entrance where the hall felt pleasantly warm again.

Once more I came back and stealthily retraced my steps... receptive to the silence... Yes, the cold was definitely concentrated around the light on the landing... By now I had goose pimples on my arms and cold shivers down my spine.

Something must have happened...RIGHT HERE!

Entering the bedroom, I sat down in the dark on the double bed facing the open door, said a prayer and started to meditate for ten minutes... a quarter of an hour. (The purpose of this exercise was not only to calm myself down. It forms a shaft of light on the Astral which ghosts can see. Protected by my spirit guide I was now deliberately inviting them to come along and take energy from this glow in order to manifest.) Although totally relaxed I was nonetheless intensely aware of the slightest change in the atmosphere.

Anything yet? Let's wait and see...

Mmmm.... A dark shadow was now slowly building up in the doorway and I could just make out the outline of a man. Motionless, I carried on watching in the stillness...

Yes, he was certainly very tall and rather forbidding. The shape was gradually becoming clearer...

Oh, dear! With a shock I noticed that the chap was hanging by his neck from the light fitting - his feet did not reach the ground. So that is why he seemed so big!...

Hey!... wait a minute! What was that at his feet?

Would you believe it... there was his faithful old dog who'd stayed all these years at his side.

The cold intensified as another shadow now joined in... From near the ceiling an elderly lady was looking down, holding out her arms to the man: his mother whom he could not see. It would have been easy for me to touch him - we were that close. At this stage my mind started to pick his thoughts: "Alexandria... the Sahara... bloody awful... had my leg blown off".

Evidently the soldier had returned from the war and found it difficult to readjust to civilian life. His artificial leg was troublesome. Gradually he'd become a recluse... not a man's man anymore... missed his mates... kept reliving dreadful battle scenes. Eventually he became so depressed that he hanged himself. And there he remained, all those years later, still mentally attached to his house, carrying on with his sad, lonely existence. It was very frustrating trying to get through to him - although I tried hard enough:

- "Look, friend, you have passed on. We're in the 1990's now... New people live in this house. Why don't you go home to the Next World? Can you see a light anywhere in the distance? If you do, then go towards it. By the way, your Mum is here. She has come to fetch you and your old dog is at your feet, wagging its tail"....

Somehow he could not understand. His shadow never moved. The gloomy atmosphere was making me shudder so perhaps it was time for a break. Still puzzled, I joined Kathleen downstairs in her cosy front room where she was reading a magazine. She looked up and I caught the glance of her very bright blue eyes. Suddenly, the penny dropped:

- "Kathy, sorry to ask... but do you take drugs"?

- "Yes, of course and so does my husband. It's nothing very strong but we both find it relaxing after a hard day - and besides, we don't drink alcohol".

- "Drugs may damage your Aura (the protective electro-magnetic waves around your body) in which case the ghost can draw freely from your own psychic energy in order to manifest. If you don't keep your lodger under control he may end up possessing you. (You have heard of Jekyll and Hyde? Well, that story relates to two souls inhabiting one body.) Spirits should come at your invitation and leave at your request. He probably never bothered the previous owners. All you have to do now is seal your Aura, give up drugs and the ghost will go away. Would you like some Spiritual Healing? It would help".

- "Yes, please. How amazing... I never knew. Tell me: have you seen the ghost? - oh, you have! Thought as much. May I go and have a look?"

We both went upstairs towards the cold atmosphere. Just inside the bedroom I asked Kathleen to lie down on the bed... a few yards away from the hanging soldier's shadow... (She couldn't see him - just as well!) Shivering, I started healing. Brrr!... It was freezing cold. Directing my hostess's thoughts, I asked her to visualise herself lying in a cool mountain stream, its clear water flowing down from her head to her feet, gently cleansing; then I proceeded to close down the seven main Chakras (or psychic centres) of her body, imagining seven bolts sliding firmly shut and finally I traced a golden light around her - all the time mentally asking for help. As I concentrated the reassuring presence of my Native American Healing guide slowly took over, overshadowing me. His soul and mine seemed to become one single unit. All doubts disappeared: my hands became strong and powerful, my arms muscled - I felt tall, confident and almost in a trance - an exhilarating experience as this Being of Light took charge of my movements. He was the transformer and I the channel conducting the healing energy. Nothing worried me anymore, nothing could harm me... still part of this world and yet floating above it...

Then, in a dream I saw the morning sun rising above the mountains in all its glory... and a white dove flying away across the blue sky... The soldier's spirit had been released... I felt elated.

Suddenly Kathleen's voice brought me back to earth:

- "Muriel, something strange has just happened. Somehow the room feels warm again... so peaceful... The ghost has gone... and I feel absolutely wonderful!"

Opening my eyes I looked around: yes, she was right, the shadows had disappeared, the ghost set free. The atmosphere was now relaxed and pleasant. Kathleen herself looked radiant as, yawning and stretching she smiled:

- "Thank God for that! Let's go downstairs and have another cup of tea".

That evening I went home on Cloud Nine. The rain was probably still pouring down - but I never noticed.

Chapter Twelve

Here, in total contrast, is

Aunt Muriel's Agony Column (Part I)

The Birds and the Bees

Over the years I have learned a lot from my sitters. You can't do my job and be prudish! All the facts of life are analysed and discussed frankly. Included is a small selection of the commonest problems. However, they are only the tip of the iceberg!

Many of my young ladies have had one - or even several - abortions. When they come for a consultation and I pick up the fact that they have lost a baby, they burst into tears, imagining the child's spirit hovering around them, pointing an accusing finger: "Mother, you KILLED me! I wanted to live!"

One person phoned from Hong-Kong: "Muriel, tell me what to do: shall I have an abortion today or not? It was a one night stand... I had too much to drink at a party... don't want the baby. But will God punish me and send me to Purgatory when I die? I am a Roman Catholic. And when I really do want a child will I be infertile?"

How could I make the decision for her? All I could advise was:

- "It's up to you, really. Everyone makes mistakes. If you decide to go ahead with the abortion then forgive yourself afterwards. Pray that the baby's soul may return to Heaven. Perhaps it will be reincarnated in your next child. What quality of life would you be able to offer that little one? Bringing up a child on your own in poverty is no fun... And in future, do go to the Family Planning Clinic."

Nowadays there is too much emphasis on sex. A teenager often believes that if she is still a virgin at 18 she will be an object of ridicule. She may be physically aroused but emotionally not ready.

When I ask: "Are you careful?" she replies: "Most of the times" or else: "I am just lucky."

- "What about Aids?"

- "I never give it a second thought. Can't spoil the rest of my life worrying about an obscure disease."

These days you can't switch on television without seeing two individuals puffing and panting in various positions. This is obviously where people get their inspiration from. Nothing is left to the imagination.

Matters have gone from one extreme to another. Gone are the days of prim and proper Doris Day who, in her films, kept her man waiting until she had a wedding ring on her finger. Now it's the extreme opposite: "I HAVE to have an orgasm. I DEMAND an orgasm... (Have half a dozen and get two free).

Talk about change! Today women wear trousers, employ men and, for entertainment, watch them stripping. Maybe in fifty years' time things will have gone full cycle when once again people will be straight-laced and the word 'lust' unmentionable.

A large percentage of my young clients go on holidays looking for romance and sex as part of the travel agency's package deal. 'Men and Sun' is all they are interested in. "Spain, ole, here I come!" (to spend all day roasting on the beach, and dancing in cattle markets called disco's at night.

- "The Alhambra, what's that? Granada? Never heard of it. But I met this dishy Aussie waiter called Barry. We had a super time together. He said he loved me... so why has he not phoned since I came back?" (Because the next planeload of tourists arrived the same day, that's why).

The number of anorexic young people I meet is worrying. They can never be slim enough. Even if she weighs six stones and looks like a skeleton a client may show me a bulge. She thinks she looks like an elephant. Surely a man likes a shapely woman - not a matchstick. And then the girl wonders why she feels so tired, weak and depressed.

Being ultra slim is fashionable in wealthy countries with a surplus of food. In underprivileged states, where people are lucky to have one meal a day, a beautiful woman is plump, showing that she can afford good food. Her large hips are an indication that she is ready for marriage and child bearing.

179

Who is your ideal partner? Most women will immediately name a film star or a famous singer. He definitely has to be tall and handsome, with slim hips, broad shoulders and blue eyes. He should also be well off. They never mention kindness, patience, loyalty... as though none of these matter. People fall in lust and call it love. The first year 'love' is in actual fact a powerful physical attraction which can subsequently turn into something deeper, but not necessarily.

When a starry eyed client tells me she has just met the man of her life I ask: "Well, what do you know about him besides the fact that he turns you on? What is he like under stress? How does he treat his mother - because that is the way he will treat you later on in life. Supposing your man goes blind or bald, or both, has an accident and is confined to a wheelchair - or, worst of all, becomes impotent - would you still want him? Because that is what love is all about, caring unconditionally, as opposed to infatuation." So if, for example, your mother (again supposing you got on well with her) was confined to a wheelchair, would it make any difference? You'd probably care for her even more".

There usually follows a long silence: "Hmm... I see what you mean... never thought of it that way."

Some people have found romance when they expected it least. Shirley was in debt up to the hilt. When the bailiff arrived to cart away her furniture he fell in love with her and she has since moved in with him.

There is a great difference between a man's and a woman's outlook on love. Subconsciously, she is searching for The Great Hero of her dreams. But where is he? In romantic novels, mostly written by women for women! She also wants him to be masterful: the idea of a primitive caveman who drags her by her hair thrills her on. Someone gentle and kind is a wimp. So, in fact, what she is looking for is a fierce warrior who will return from the battle-field bringing her romance and passion.

However, the average chap is only passionate while making love. Afterwards, sitting up in bed with a cup of coffee, she expects him to pay her compliments instead of which he switches on the television set, smiling contentedly: - "Great! I am just in time for the Big Match." (Of course, there are exceptions!)

I have had the most incredible situations here when for example, a man brought along his wife one week and his mistress the next - neither aware of each other's existence.

180

Many of my male clients are worried about their sexual prowess. They ask the oddest questions: - "What is the average size of a man's penis?"... "How do I compare with other men?"... "How long should a performance take?" (They think I can read the answers in the cards!) Their queries are made in sincerity, because they are genuinely worried and feel too embarrassed to ask anyone else. There is no shortage of informative books available which I recommend but at a later date their usual excuse is:

- "The cashier was a pretty young girl and I bought a science fiction book instead."

Women are often too embarrassed to discuss their emotional needs with their partner. And if life revolves exclusively around work and the home a relationship will become stale. Sex will be just another boring chore together with the ironing and the week-end shopping.

A mature man who suddenly, for no apparent reason, has an affair with a woman half his age is trying to prove to himself that he is still young and virile. He is afraid of growing old so when a young person has a crush on him it gives a great boost to his ego. He seldom leaves his wife unless they are enemies already. His secret affair is exciting, livening up a boring life.

It's only when the girlfriend expects her lover to move in with her that problems arise. He has no intention of leaving the security of his home, his established routine nor his children. Even if he and his wife sleep in separate bedrooms she is still a friend and, let's face it, he has the best of both worlds. The same story is valid for women too.

Kim, a mother of four, produced a photograph of her lover: an old boy, at least twice her age, who was a long distance lorry driver. When he told his wife that he was going away on business, he was actually travelling as far as the next road to stay with Kim.

- "His wife is an old battle axe. Tell me: is he going to leave her for me?"

Believe it or not, a chance in a million, the following week a lady in her sixties came for a reading and produced... the same passport photograph of this vintage Romeo! I couldn't believe it!

- "Please tell me... I suspect my husband of having an affair with that young hussy down the road..."

181

Who had given them my telephone number? How I managed to keep a straight face I shall never know.

Similarly, when two people decide to divorce, they may suddenly miss each other:

- "It was all my fault"....

- "No, it was mine."

So they agree to have another go. Everything is wonderful for a few months and she becomes pregnant. But then they start getting on each other's nerves again. Nothing has changed: they go back to the same irritating habits. Arguments flare up and eventually they will separate for good. Then they remember: why did they divorce in the first place? Because they are totally incompatible.

What then is Love? It is caring for each other's well-being. You should be able to sit down together with, perhaps a glass of wine or a cup of tea and just enjoy each other's company without even thinking of sex. Neither partner should suffocate the other; you must have your own space and the freedom to pursue separate hobbies.

Love means trust and mutual respect, laughter and talking differences over in a relaxed way, going out together regularly even if it is only for a walk in the park - in fact, it's being best friends.

But let's move on. I now wish to mention the subject of nuisance phone calls. These are an irritating time waster of which I get my fare share. After a while one becomes immune! The chat lines have taken over, offering a great service to perverts and I am very grateful. However, some men still ask outright:

- "How much do you charge for sex?" The answer is invariably:

- "More than you can afford!" as I slam the phone down.

At the end of a reading, one of my clients, a bald headed, potbellied Mediterranean commented:

- "Yes, the clairvoyance was O.K...."

(Looking me up and down): "Hmm... you ain't no spring chicken no more, but I ain't fussy neither. Tell you what: I'll come back on Friday with a bottle of wine.

We'll have a few drinks before getting down to 'The Business'." (My body for the price of a bottle of wine!) Resisting the impulse to throw the contents of my coffee cup at his bald patch I declined politely and got rid of him as fast as possible!

What makes some men think a medium is a Psychic Madam who runs a brothel? One person offered me £60 to come and masturbate in front of me. He was serious and thought his offer was too good to refuse. A friend laughed when I told her the story:

- "Now let's see. Is it £60 for ten minutes (in which case it's a bargain) or for half an hour, ha-ha!" while her sister shuddered: "Ugh! Just imagine having to pick up all that mess from the carpet."

Sometimes the calls are funny. For example the young yuppie:

- "Is that Muriel?"

- "Yes."

- "Muriel, the medium?"

- "That's right."

- "Tell me: what services do you offer?"

- "Well, what services did you have in mind?"

- "I want a massage... ALL OVER!" (Yes, I knew exactly what he wanted!)

- "Sorry, I am a medium, not a prostitute!"

After a short silence, he asked:

- "What's the difference?" (What! He didn't know the difference between a medium and a prostitute!)

In my best undertaker's voice I whispered:

- "I bring you messages from spirits... BEYOND THE GRAVE...Is that what you want?"

After another prolonged silence, he answered nervously:

- "Er, well, no... sorry... must have the wrong number"... before ringing off in a hurry.

The memory of this story still makes me chuckle today.

Most obscene callers are jokers in bad taste or misfits of society who can't find a relationship. They enjoy fantasising and frightening lonely women. It gives them a feeling of power when the person reacts. As a rule they are harmless, sneaky cowards (unless, of course, they know the woman personally) but British Telecom's new tracing system is very helpful. My son's deep voice booming: "Hello!" does wonders too as, after some hesitation the caller rings off.

Some people just want to unburden their guilty secrets. Within reason I listen, time permitting. If a person is genuinely distraught I will do my best to help and advise, or put them in touch with the appropriate Helpline.

When the phone rings I never know what to expect. Maybe it's an elderly woman who wants a chat because she feels lonely or else I am confronted with the most astonishing anonymous confessions:

- "My wife goes to Bingo every Friday night. While she is away I pop into bed with my little daughter. Can you help...?"

My mind goes blank. H...E...L...P! What do I answer? Telling the man what I think of him is a waste of time. I feel like suggesting:

- "Why don't you go to Bingo too?" but instead I say:

- "Oh, dear! And I gather you have sex with her?"

- "Yes, of course. But tell me: why is she so reluctant? My little girl is most unreasonable."

- "I bet she is, poor thing. And I suppose your wife doesn't know?"

- "No, that is our little secret."

- "Do you love your daughter?"

- "Of course, I care for her very much."

184

- "Then you must realise that you are ruining her life, putting her off sex for good, together with the chance of ever having a boyfriend, getting married, having children..." (Help again! What do I say now?)... "When did you first start having intercourse?"

- "When she was six months old. But it wasn't much fun. She was always screaming."

- "You need help, you know. What you are doing is wrong. You must know otherwise you wouldn't have called me. Here is the Samaritan's phone number. They are better qualified at dealing with your problem than I am. And it's totally anonymous - no, they won't call the police."

Ringing off, I feel shaken and sick. Did I say the right thing? The man obviously realised he needed help so I gave him the Samaritans' phone number - and the best of luck to them!

Incest is very common. It's just kept secret. I have had several other similar phone calls. As a mother, it alway gives me a shock but I try and analyse the problem without emotions. Screaming at the chap would achieve nothing. He'd only put the phone down. Occasionally a client remembers being assaulted in childhood by a relative. Invariably the experience has left an indelible mark which can never be forgotten.

Rape is another subject discussed anonymously on the phone. For the first ten minutes my callers beat about the bush. They feel uneasy and as I sympathise, they gradually unwind, coming to the real purpose of their call. Then slowly they tell me the story, in every lurid detail. I am the first person they have confided in although the assault happened perhaps two months earlier. They feel dirty, ashamed - as though it's their fault. You'd think it all happened less than half an hour ago. They are confused, in a state of shock, as they carry on with their daily business pretending nothing has happened.

Listening, I forget about the housework and any other task... it can wait. An hour later they are more poised, seeing things differently. Hopefully they will have a test at the clinic and go to the police. I encourage them to phone Rape Crisis - a special number where they will receive advice and help, and to call me again anytime. What more can I do?

People can be so cruel to each other. And what about animals? They can't pick up the phone and dial the RSPCA to lodge a formal complaint. For instance a neighbour down the road had gone on holidays leaving her kitten locked up without food or water. The milkman informed me of the fact, adding: "What a shame, the poor little thing has been miaowing near the door for the past week. His cries are getting weaker." It was a hot July day too.

Going around the flat I called through the letterbox. The little creature came readily, looking at me pitifully. The neighbours were not interested: "Don't want to get involved. None of my business. Yes, it's a pity, the kitten will soon be dead. Pretty little animal too."

So it was left to me to call the R.S.P.C.A. The inspector on the telephone was very helpful: "Put some ice cubes through the letterbox and cat food if you don't mind getting some." He was there in no time and took over. He put a notice on the door and a thread across so that no one could go in without breaking it. He asked me to carry on putting ice cubes through the letterbox while he would supply food every morning. After 48 hours, as the woman had not returned, he called the police who broke in and rescued the kitten.

Later on the inspector phoned me to say that the kitten was in good health and would be found a welcoming home miles away and that the woman would be taken to court.

But how many other animals are not so lucky?

Aunt Muriel's Agony Column (Part II)

Gay People

My regular clients include gay people. Many of the gorgeous, handsome air stewards who come and see me are homosexual - although they may have all the women chasing after them. Most of these men are shy, gentle and creative so they make good actors, singers, psychics, dancers, carers - in fact any of the professions requiring sensitivity.

At first they are reserved as they sit down drinking their tea in silence. Once they realise that it doesn't bother me whether they are homosexual or not, and that I accept them as they are, they start to relax. Who am I to pass judgement anyway?

The Bible and society dictate that we should be heterosexual. So we are brought up and conditioned to believe that this is the norm. When I was a teenager homosexuality was never discussed openly and there was no Gay Rights Association in existence either.

In the Ancient World homosexuality was often regarded as being as natural as heterosexuality. There is much ignorance and prejudice on this subject and I am not going to weigh its pros and cons here. I only wish to mention some of the gays I have met.

As in nature nothing is clear cut. If, for example, there are thousands of varieties of butterflies instead of one standard species, does the same not apply to people and their emotions?

Also I wonder whether there is a possibility of a woman's soul being trapped inside a man's body and the other way around. If I were born a man I would be miserable, and still behave like a woman.

Among homosexuals too there are those who are feminine and others who aren't while some are so masculine, like Lawrence of Arabia, that they prefer men's company. My bisexual clients don't mind whether they find a male or female partner. In truth, many people are attracted to both sexes - I suppose it gives them more scope!

Love between two consulting adult gays is their own business, as long as they don't perform in front of me or harm anyone else - and I don't have to pay tax on it. "Live and let live" is my motto.

The average gay client either accepts himself as he is or hides the fact. Finding a steady partner is not easy at the best of times but for a homosexual it is even more difficult. He may be attracted to a Mr Muscles who regularly lets him down and has several other boyfriends already - or perhaps his relationship is with a prosperous businessman, possibly married, who wants a bit of secret excitement on the side. So the poor dejected lover spends hours waiting for that elusive phone call. ("Don't call us, we'll call you.") But I have also met some who have settled down and live happily together.

Many homosexuals love children and would make good fathers which complicates the issue further. A little boy told me the other day: "I live with my two Mums!"

It seemed a bit odd but the boy is evidently happy with the situation. (If you had been brought up by two caring women would you have complained?) In an ideal world children need both a mother and a father but they are better off with one single parent than with two who continually argue. In his case the boy had two devoted mothers.

The other evening when I answered the telephone I heard a man's voice sobbing hysterically down the line:

- "Can you help me? I love my boyfriend very much but he beats me up! Although I wash his clothes, cook nice meals and keep the house tidy he still hits me when he comes home. I am SO depressed. What shall I do?" (How about standing up to the chap or leaving him?) I could just imagine my caller wearing a frilly apron and wringing his manicured hands in despair... It sounded like an extract from the film "La cage aux folles." Poor fellow! I did feel sorry for him.

An acquaintance of mine suddenly left his wife and four children for another man. All too often these hasty arrangements don't work out as Ray was soon to discover at his own cost: he missed his kids, his home - if not the wife - and ended up losing everything including the lover.

Why does a middle aged married woman suddenly decide to leave her husband and settle down with another woman? Because:

- Subconsciously she may already be bisexual: her present partner shows her no affection and takes her for granted; she has become part of the fixtures and fittings.

The husband may be a workaholic - or perhaps he disappears every weekend to play golf. Now that the children have left home she feels bored, lonely and rejected. Then she meets someone who cares and treats her with kindness and consideration. So, welcoming the chance of a new life, she packs her bags and tells her husband to cook his own meals in future.

A young lesbian Maori fell in love with me. She was a pretty, plump thing with dark, doleful eyes. It was all rather embarrassing. In a state of depression she came for a reading, unloaded all her problems and then decided I was the Woman of her life. She phoned every day:

- "Would you like to have dinner with me this evening? I can offer you roast chicken... and anything else you would like. You could stay the night too..."

The innuendoes were far from subtle. It was a difficult situation: if I upset her she could have a nervous breakdown and may even become suicidal.

But in the end, I had to tell her, as kindly as possible, that although I very much appreciated her friendship I could not respond to her advances. The poor girl was terribly upset, crying down the phone:

- "But, Muriel I LOVE YOU you SO much!"

- "Sorry, I am not attracted to other women. You are such a nice person. One day you will meet someone who will really appreciate you."

She never phoned again. I wonder what happened to her.

Another woman I can't forget in a hurry - one of my first clients in fact - came for a reading because she was upset over a broken love affair. Jan was tall and blonde with bright hazel eyes. Trying to reassure her that she would meet Mr Right was a waste of time. In fact, the mere mention of men irritated her. She kept deriding them whilst looking me up and down with a hungry, excited look on her face that made me feel rather uneasy. Being still relatively green at the time it was only after her departure that the penny finally dropped.

When puzzled, I commented: "Why was this such a difficult reading? It was almost impossible to get through to her."

Nathan replied: "I hope you did not tell her that she was going to meet a new boyfriend! Your lady was a lesbian, Mum, didn't you know? You are supposed to be psychic!"

Of course! I could have kicked myself. Oh, dear! And there I was trying to convince her that she was going to meet another man. (Sorry: can't win 'em all!)

Over the years I have met homosexuals, bisexuals, transsexuals - you name it - also a few young men who are not sure whether they are gay or not: perhaps they went to an all-boys college and had homosexual experiences. But that does not necessarily mean that they are going to be attracted solely to their own sex for the rest of their lives.

The Submissive Cleaners

On a number of occasions I have been contacted by men applying for a cleaning job. Although I protest: "But I don't run a Domestic Agency, try someone else!" they persevere:

- "Please let me come and scrub your kitchen floor, wash your windows, shampoo your carpets, clean the oven..."

They are prepared to travel from the other side of London and do all this work free of charge! (Sounds too good to be true. What's the catch?) Some of them enjoy being scolded severely while they work. (Oh, no! Not by me, sorry!) They find it quite titillating. One man, a solicitor, wished to polish my shoes and lie at my feet as payment for cleaning my flat. ("My husband wouldn't approve" I assured him).

Three times I have also been asked by anonymous Phillipino women who could barely speak English:

- "Muriel, I have just arrived in England. May I come and live with you? Would you like a slave?"

Shocked, I replied hastily:

- "NO, THANK YOU! Why don't you try the Domestic Agencies in the Yellow Pages?"

190

- "But it's YOU I want to be with. I want to be YOUR slave! Let me bring you breakfast in bed, brush your hair, wash your clothes, help you get dressed, give you a massage..."

- "NO, THANK YOU!"

They felt very hurt at being rejected. But surely they did not expect every medium to be interested in hiring a slave? Their insistence was disquieting...

Recently I mentioned these callers to a Phillipino lady. She smiled: "But, Muriel, did you not realise that your would-be slaves were men - not women?"

- "But I could have sworn that they were women... the soft, feminine voice..."

She laughed: "No, no... they were definitely men!"

In retrospect I now realise that she was right...

Transvestites

Another subject altogether is Transvestites - heterosexual men who enjoy dressing up as women. It can't be much fun for the wife watching her husband wearing a wig and make-up - in fact it must have been quite a shock for one of my sitters who came home to find her man dressed up in her underwear. She could not take it and is now divorced. Some wives are angels of patience as they try to understand why an otherwise perfect husband wishes to dress up as a woman. They even buy them suitable clothes and show them how to apply make-up. Others find it quite exciting and actually encourage their partner to wear outrageous outfits.

Another man complained that his girlfriend was most unreasonable:

- "She won't let me try on her clothes - nor even a little of her lipstick. In fact she has just stormed out, slamming the door behind her. I really don't understand why she reacts this way..."

Those transvestites I have met are kind, genuine people. They are heterosexual and just enjoy dressing up as women. We all have both masculine and feminine tendencies: women may be very domineering and tough men can cry over a soppy love story. Not all transvestites cross-dress, some are quite happy just wearing women's underwear underneath their suit. They are obsessed with silky,

191

frilly lingerie and will spend hours discussing the subject whereas a woman buys underwear as required and then forgets about it. Her make up is subtle, just enough to enhance her natural looks. A transvestite tends to slap on the warpaint until he looks like a character out of a pantomime.

People are becoming more tolerant. In some large stores beauticians will show a man how to apply makeup. Centres have been established where these people can meet and cross-dress to their heart's content in a controlled environment.

John is a man who phones me regularly when he feels low. After twenty years of marriage his wife went off with his best friend. He has three daughters and several grandchildren. John is a bricklayer. He confided that when he comes home from the building site he changes into pretty feminine clothes. They make him feel good. He looks at himself in the mirror and suddenly becomes depressed and lonely - no, he certainly wouldn't go out dressed like that. What would the neighbours think? The first time he phoned I couldn't resist asking:

- "And what are you wearing now, John?"

- "At the moment my name is Jane and I am in a lovely pink bridesmaid's dress with a big bow and rosy satin underwear."

I had a vision of the comedian Les Dawson dressed up as one of the Ugly Sisters in "*Cinderella*" and could picture a muscled man wearing a pretty party dress, a large blonde wig, false eyelashes, luminous blue eye shadow... stiletto heeled shoes.

When he called again, I asked:

- "What are you wearing today, Jane?"

- "My wife's wedding dress with her white veil. Wish you could see me... I look ever so pretty!"

John (or Jane when cross-dressing) seems a very nice, gentle person who wouldn't harm a fly. I feel so sorry for him locked up in his lonely world. Why can't he go jogging around the block instead or do something more constructive? Although I gave him the address of the Transvestite magazine and the nearest club where he would meet others on his wavelength he refuses to help himself. His dearest wish is to come and see me for a reading. If I allow it, he would then change in the bathroom and come out in a party frock. (But, unfortunately for him, I am not interested).

Years ago we had a neighbour who was married to an elderly woman twice his age. In the morning I would see a tarty blonde woman leaving their home - until I realised that it was the husband in a miniskirt and a blonde wig. At seven-thirty he would do a handstand in front of his house displaying his goods to anyone who cared to look. Soon the neighbours across the road noticed him from their front window. The news spread like wildfire and other residents, still in their dressing gowns, came crowding in at the window, encouraging the chap with their witty comments. Indeed it became a "Room with a View" and the man loved all the attention. He was the talk of the street - until one unsporty neighbour called the police who carted him away - and that was the end of the free entertainment.

One of my clients had both sexes. She had a bust and shaved her beard. She was waiting for an operation to have the superfluous part removed. Her parents wanted her to be a man but she felt more feminine than masculine.

- "What shall I do? My father is very domineering and if I don't obey his orders he will be furious."

- "It's YOUR body - and YOUR life. YOU make the decision."

She was gentle, sensitive and so lonely through no fault of her own. I wanted to reassure her: "I CARE!"

Over the years it has become much easier for me to pinpoint the root of a problem and to discuss it in a relaxed, matter-of-fact way.

Take, for example, the case of George B., a distinguished stockbroker. (With his good looks and public school accent he would have made a splendid Shakespearean character). He had everything going for him: a great career, an expensive house, a devoted wife and three delightful children.

- "But why", he sighed, "does my wife irritate me so much? Yes, give her her due, she is pleasant and dresses smartly. But she BORES me! I don't find her attractive anymore. In fact, I resent her even being near me."

It all seemed perfectly reasonable. On the surface here was the classical story of a couple who, after years of marriage, had nothing left in common. And yet... Scrutinising those pale blue eyes and thick silvery hair I pondered in silence... Hmmm... something did not add up. Finally I decided to take the plunge as I asked somewhat hesitantly: Forgive me... but have you ever thought you might be bisexual?"

Startled, he jumped up: "ME? what do you mean? But, carry on. I must confess you are on the right track."

- "I feel that you could be suppressing your real sexual nature and that is why you resent your wife so much".

- "You are right. I owe you the truth: although I am not bisexual I am, in fact, a transvestite but it would be a disgrace to my family if anyone found out. Just imagine my son telling his school friends: 'My Daddy dresses up as a woman!' So I have vowed never to give in to this weakness and start cross-dressing."

- "Listen. Be reasonable. Your feelings of guilt and frustration seem to make everyone else's life a misery. Your poor wife suffers. You probably snap at your children. Why not contact the Beaumont Society where you could go and cross dress to your heart's content in a safe, controlled environment? No one else need know. You simply disappear for a few hours and return home feeling relaxed and cheerful. And everyone will benefit! After all you are not harming anyone by dressing up as a woman".

He thought things over in silence for a while then looked up and gave me a big smile: "I have been carrying this weight around for many years and you have solved my problem in a matter of minutes"...

George went home with a spring in his step.

And so I carry on day after day trying to help people sort out their problems... an endless flow. My aim is to give them hope and a new sense of direction without criticising or moralising.

By now I have heard so many extraordinary confessions that nothing surprises me anymore! And yet I can't expect to please everyone, however hard I try. For example, I could give an almost identical reading to two people. The first one may be delighted and the second totally disappointed. I can't win. Give a spiritual message to a materialistic person and it's a total waste of time and effort.

It certainly takes all sorts to make this world...

Chapter Thirteen

Louise

New neighbours had moved in. Cyril (The same Cyril already mentioned earlier) was a tall, middle-aged, preoccupied looking man in a grey suit. Lou, his wife, a pleasant woman, chatted amiably whenever we met in the stairs. On one occasion she smiled happily:

- "We were married recently. He is my second husband, you know... such a kind, considerate man."

She was obviously in love with him. Indeed, from time to time I would see the aloof Cyril coming home with a large bunch of flowers. It was nice to see two middle-aged people who cared so much for each other.

From time to time Lou would announce excitedly: "Cyril just phoned from work. He told me not to bother cooking because he is taking me out for a show in the West-End and a meal afterwards."

A few months later, although still smiling, my neighbour seemed to have lost her sparkle. Her thick brown hair was lanky. She confided:

- "Somehow I don't feel so well these days... always tired. I am under the hospital for tests."

Every time I met her she seemed paler and I was becoming rather concerned.

Then Cyril, who so far had only nodded "Hello", suddenly stopped me in the street:

- "My wife has cancer. She was admitted into hospital yesterday. Thought I'd better let you know."

To tell the truth I hardly knew either of them so, not wishing to intrude, I kept myself apart.

Cyril

A fortnight later I had just gone to bed when suddenly an unexpected sound in the room made me sit up bold straight.

SOMEONE WAS MOVING ABOUT!

In the darkness a bright light was shining at the foot of my bed. Rubbing my eyes I stared in astonishment for there in front of me stood Lou.

But how could this be possible? As far as I knew she was still alive! Yet this was definitely the same person. She looked radiant in the blinding light as though many film projectors were being focused on her. Once more Lou's hair

196

Cyril's wife Louise who stood at the foot of my bed waving good-bye three days before her death

was thick and glossy. She wore a stylish green dress and seemed perfectly healthy.

Yet at this moment in time my neighbour was in hospital - still breathing - although probably very thin and ill.

It was all a bit of a shock - being jerked out of my sleep to face the elegant ghost of a person who was still alive.

Smiling gently she said:

- "Well, I'm off now. Muriel. You will keep an eye on Cyril, won't you because otherwise he will go to pieces. You know about these things - but he doesn't - and that is why I have come to you. Bye for now!"

The light started to lose its brightness... slowly fading away until I was back in the dark. Lou too had vanished... She really must have worried about her husband to come and see me, yet I had never even told her that I was a medium... Perplexed I went to sleep.

Three days later the door bell rang. It was Cyril, looking pale and lost. He just stood there staring vacantly. On an impulse I said:

 - "It's alright... I know. She came to say good-bye three days ago."

197

Cyril looked startled; his mouth dropped open in amazement:

- "What do you mean... she visited you? Lou was ill in hospital for the past fortnight. She only died a few hours ago, so how could you possibly know?"

The poor man probably thought I was mad! My fault for being impulsive. Touching his arm briefly I added:

- "Do come in. I'll make you a cup of coffee."

Dazed, my neighbour followed me indoors. He sat down all hunched up on a kitchen chair, staring at the floor, his mind in a turmoil.

- "Do you take sugar, Cyril?"

- "We'd only been married eight months..." he answered.

- "I am so sorry about your wife... but believe you me I DID see her. She looked fit and well. Life goes on in another dimension. You will meet again one day..."

It was so difficult to choose the right words. Very little got through to him as he was in a state of shock. Finally, not knowing what else to say to reassure him I asked:

- "May I borrow your watch, Cyril?"

He handed the article over. I had not realised how receptive my neighbour was for as soon as I started, the clairvoyance was flowing:

- "Tell me, who was Mrs Rose?"

Puzzled, he answered:

- "That was my landlady, years ago."

- "Well, she is here with your Auntie Gert - the lady who liked Gin..."

By now Cyril was paying full attention:

- "Yes, Auntie Gert. I remember her well. After her death we found a cupboard full of empty Gin bottles..."

198

- And all those soldiers with a pint in their hand... your wartime friends. Did you know that only two of you came out of Greece alive?" (Then I mentioned a few names which he recognised.)

My guest was fascinated. He wanted to know more. Over the following weeks he went from one Spiritualist Church to another. Everywhere he was given messages proving undoubtedly that his wife was alive and well in another dimension. They were of great comfort to him. For example, on their wedding anniversary Cyril bought an orchid which he stuck to Lou's photograph. The same evening in church the medium announced:

- "I have a smiling lady here with beautiful dark hair who assures me she is your wife. She likes the orchid! She is also saying that you will find a message inside the frame."

As soon as he got home Cyril opened the frame and removed the photograph. As he did so, a small slip of paper fell onto the table. Shaken, he recognised his wife's familiar handwriting. The short message read: "Cyril. All my love - always."

My neighbour has since retired from work. He still finds clairvoyance fascinating. He is a kind, friendly man (the same person, mentioned before, who accompanied me to Gordon's funeral). This is the story as he remembers it:-

"It was Sunday, 10th February. My second wife, Lou, had passed away at 3.15 that morning. I really don't know what I felt like - that last night had been spent at her bedside holding her hand and talking to her although she was unconscious.

On getting back to my flat I was walking up and down, wearing a hole in the carpet. Lou and I had only been married for eight months and in that time I had practically no contact with our neighbours. But Lou had spoken to Muriel Renard, the lady in the flat below ours so I went down to tell her the news. I rang her bell. She came to the door and said:

- "Oh, I am sorry you've lost her. I knew she was going: she came to me three days ago and told me so."

I looked at her and thought what on earth she was talking about. Lou had been in hospital for at least two weeks.

Muriel then invited me into her kitchen saying:

- "I am sorry, I've shocked you. Come in. I'll make you a cup of coffee."

I sat there, far away in my mind. She then said:

- "That's a nice watch you have. May I look at it?"

I gave her the watch and for the next hour sat and listened to my life story. She was talking about things that no being on earth would know anything about but me. When she had finished, I got up in a daze. It was then that she told me that she was a medium and if at any time I wanted company or someone to talk to I should go to a Spiritualist church. This I did. Ten days after my wife had passed I found myself in Wimbledon Spiritualist Church where I received a message from my late wife of such content that it could have come from nowhere else. Wonderful!

I thank Muriel for that first link and am now a practising healer. Great things have happened.

Cyril A Setchell.

All Nationalities...

My home is like Piccadilly Circus. The average crowd waiting for the train trickles through my flat: secretaries, students, tourists, journalists, solicitors, pensioners, actresses, traffic wardens, businessmen, civil servants, dancers, musicians etc.

One must enjoy turning one's home into a public gallery as there is very little privacy left. Some arrive an hour early while I am in the middle of a meal or two hours late when I am in the bath. They get me out of bed in the middle of the night without apologies expecting an instant solution to their problems. Sometimes I am asleep in the morning when the door bell rings with someone demanding a reading.

They come with their pain, their hopes and ambitions seeking reassurance. Maybe the colour of their skin varies but inside people have the same emotions and hurts. They are searching high and low for this elusive HAPPINESS, perfect LOVE and a carefree, prosperous life.

The following notes are made haphazardly as I recall various clients. It would be incorrect to generalise, stating that ALL the inhabitants of a specific country are

200

the same for, of course, they are not so. These are just a few of the people I remember. Some countries have different customs to mine which I noted with interest. (For example, a Norwegian client told me that herring and rice pudding are a delicacy on her Christmas menu.) It would be impossible for me to take you on a quick trip around the world pointing out the various inhabitants and their traditions. But I feel privileged to have such an interesting life and so many friends.

Perhaps I should start with the Anglo-Saxon as London is now my home. I always wished to live here and am quite happy to reside on the outskirts of the town, both near the centre and at the same time not far from the countryside. There is nothing prettier than the gardens of Hampton Court Palace in the Spring when the lawns are full of daffodils and the trees are pink with blossom. I enjoy strolling along the Thames in Kingston watching the swans stretching their wings and the boats sailing by.

Reigate Hill is another favourite haunt when the woods are resplendent with bluebells. On the other hand I can be in London in no time to attend lectures, visit galleries, meet friends or go shopping.

Living in England I have discovered the following differences with my own background. An English outlook on life is inherited in one's genes. Its influence has taught me to calm down and speak more slowly although I still find it a struggle not to gesticulate while illustrating a point! So this is how the British built an Empire! Everyone remained cool under stress... It was just another game of cricket. Their dry humour is different too.

In the Old School - and probably still today - the middle class sent their sons - and often their daughters too - to boarding school at the age of seven. The children were out on their own at a tender age. I find this incomprehensible as I was brought up with warmth and constant attention, being able to run home to my parents to tell them all about my successes and failures at school.

Another point of astonishment is all the sports and competitive activities organised by the teachers. One wonders when the children ever had time to study at all.

Now I realise that the boys were brought up as the descendants of knights-in-armour. The games are a legacy of jousting, falconry etc. and, in fact, the young men were being prepared for the battle-field. They were not allowed to cry or show any emotions and that is why today adult Englishmen still find it difficult to express their feelings. When I am given a present I exclaim with delight whereas a middle class English person will simply say: "Thank you." If asked: "Do you like this gift?" they will smile: "Yes, it's fine." It does not mean that they are not thrilled - they just can't show their emotions.

Children of the wealthy were brought up by a nanny who dutifully took them to say "good morning" and "good night" to their parents twice a day. They ate separately upstairs. So Mamma lavished all her love on her dogs and her horses. Those children must have grown up with complexes. I can understand people loving animals but surely their children need even more affection.

The stereotype public school Englishman with an affected accent is slowly disappearing together with bowler hats and striped trousers. Today most people own a television set showing how the rest of the world live. We have become a multiracial society who go abroad on holidays. So people are more open minded. Unfortunately, colourful national costumes are fast disappearing too to be replaced by tee-shirts and jeans.

Knowledge of the Anglo-Saxon temperament has helped me a lot in my readings. How many times have I advised couples to hug each other when they come home, to be more demonstrative and to communicate more! Just saying: "You look really nice in that outfit" makes all the difference.

Working class Londoners are practical and tough because it has always been the survival of the fittest. You know where you stand with them: if they like you they accept you. They can become excellent friends. I have also discovered that in general poor people are more generous than wealthy ones.

Some of my sitters are restless, going for treks up the Himalayas, a rucksack on their back. Others prefer to join an expedition through African jungles travelling the cheapest way in an old, overcrowded lorry that is likely to break down at any moment in the middle of the swamps. Being young they feel invincible! Snakes and spiders only bite others. They think me unreasonable when I advise:

- "Take out a medical insurance. Only go somewhere where you are within reach of a hospital. For example, if you are in the middle of the Australian bush, that's fine for in an emergency you could easily be rescued by helicopter.

In actual fact, many of my clients go abroad because they think the grass will be greener overseas. They are simply running away from a broken affair or a boring job. I suggest:

- "Stay put and solve your problems first. If you are not happy at home the chances are you won't be content anywhere else in the world either. Certainly, travelling is a great experience. It broadens your outlook, but don't just pack your bags to escape from your problems because eventually you will have to return to them. In another country the scenery may be different but people also struggle to make a living: they are born, get married, raise a family and have bills to pay. Find peace of mind first and then, if you still feel like travelling, by all means go ahead. At least, at home you have your roots, your family and friends. If you are already lonely before your departure - what chances do you stand in unfamiliar surroundings? The more you drift around the world the more solitary you will feel.

More women book an appointment than men. Why? Because they are more interested in clairvoyance. Men tend to laugh it off (albeit rather uneasily) but when they are really in trouble they forget their prejudices and come to see me. ("I don't usually believe in this hocus-pocus but...") Occasionally I meet a man who is spiritually aware, and it's a pleasure to give him a reading.

It would be difficult for me to write about the various Europeans I meet because they are too close to my own background. I do feel sorry for the ladies from Bosnia and other war torn areas who are anxious about their relatives. It is not an easy task trying to give them hope and encouragement.

American tourists who come to me are very nice. They love History, ancient buildings and (the store) Harrods. "If ever you are in America, Muriel, just call and see us."

I have met a descendant of a famous Indian Chief who, along with hundreds of others, is searching for the deeds of his ancestors' land. But I have also met an Englishman who is just as interested in tracing his own remote American ancestor, a valiant cavalryman who took part in a battle... and yes, you've guessed... was awarded a piece of land in return for his bravery.

Young Australians and New Zealanders I give readings to are friendly, outgoing and sporty. As there is no class distinction in their country, they are relaxed and treat everyone as equals. Most of my visitors are either nannies, secretaries or else they work in a pub or restaurant. (I was told that in Australia it's the other way around: the waitresses usually come from such exotic places as Tooting Broadway or Wandsworth Common). Whereas an Englishman's home is his castle where he spends the long winter months Aussies enjoy their leisure time out in the sunshine on the beach. So they find it easy to talk to perfect strangers as though they had known them all their lives.

Aussies and Kiwis are keen to visit the whole world and make lots of friends at the same time. They like pubs and wine bars. They are happy-go-lucky with a big smile on their faces. They carry a little of their Australian sunshine with them. A favourite haunt of theirs is the Church where they meet on a Sunday. (Believe it or not, it's a converted church in Kings Cross that has been turned into a swinging pub.)

New Zealanders have a funny accent. For example:

- "My boyfriend and I fart a lot."

- "I beg your pardon? What do you eat? Baked beans?"

- "No, no. We don't git on - we fart (fight) a lot."

Another time it was:

- "Do you type?"

- Yes, I do. But why do you wish to know about my secretarial skills?"

- "No... I want to bring a type (tape) along to record the reading."

When a sitter told me she was going for a curse I was intrigued... until I guessed she meant a course.

Some young ladies come to London to keep up with their globetrotting friends. They are homesick but would hate to admit to it. If they could swallow their pride they would be on the next plane back home.

A neighbour's son spent six months in Australia. Upon his return he was delighted to tell me about his trip Down Under.

- "And guess what"...

- "Yes?"

- "In the bush, right in the middle of nowhere I met a couple and - wait for it! - the girl had been to see you for a reading! In Sydney, I would have accepted the remote possibility - but this was miles away from anywhere."

He was very impressed (and so was I!). His mother found it all very entertaining.

Many young Indian ladies who come and see me have the same problem: they are brought up in England with Western ideas but their parents expect them to adhere to Eastern customs.

The most common cause of conflict is the Arranged Marriage. When the parents decide it's time for their daughter to get married they start looking around for a suitable match. They have saved up to give her a dowry and an expensive wedding. So they select carefully with the help of friends and relatives. The girl is introduced to a few eligible bachelors from her own background and caste. If she agrees to marry one of them then the wedding takes place within the next six months. On the other hand her husband may also come gift wrapped as a surprise on her wedding day. These arrangements often work out surprisingly well, friendship turning into love.

It's when they don't that the wife comes for a sitting, crying in despair:

- "Chandra comes home and plays with our son ignoring me completely. He is never interested in making love. We sleep in separate bedrooms. I think he is still in love with someone else."

- "My husband is such a difficult man. We have two children. The problem is that I am in love with his brother whose arranged marriage is also unhappy. The way he looks at me I know he cares too but nothing can ever come of it. It's so depressing!

I met a beautiful, graceful Indian lady who had been married off to a man twice her age. She even brought her husband along because he wouldn't let her go anywhere on her own. He was a well-to-do lawyer with plenty of money but little else to recommend him. She found him as exciting as yesterday's cold chupatee and wished she had become a nun instead.

So, all in all, when parents inform their daughter that it's time for her to get married she either submits to their authority or packs her bags and leaves home. Families are closely knit so if she defies them and goes out with the boy she met at college whom they find unsuitable she will be ostracised - father threatening to kill her and mother threatening to kill herself. What is the girl to do? She knows that if her romance turns sour she will end up a very lonely person, rejected by her relatives.

Kumar's parents arranged his marriage. It was a great, expensive affair. They never listened to his pleas, dismissing the fact that he already had an English girlfriend. The wedding went ahead as planned after which Kumar immediately returned to his sweetheart without even consummating the marriage. The whole event was a disgrace to the family.

The ladies are softly spoken. They never run for a bus. They look beautiful in their colourful sarees and remain calm and dignified at all times.

On the whole Indians are respectable and hardworking. Gita, a greengrocer's wife and mother of three, tells me that she gets up at 5 o'clock in the morning and does all the housework first before opening the shop. She is at work from 8.30 a.m. until 6.30p.m., six days a week. Her mother-in-law, who lives with the family, prepares their evening meal. Although I am sure it all helps to pay the bills she has no time for leisure or hobbies. She lives to work. These customs stem back from the days when there was no pension and people had to to save every Rupee for their old age. In India people have several children whose duty it will be to look after them when they are old.

Several Indian and Pakistani people I met - both male and female - went home on holidays unsuspectingly and returned with a partner. Their wedding had been secretly arranged and they found it impossible to stand up to family pressure. But what about the poor girl who comes from her village straight to England? She has such high expectations, marrying a sophisticated cosmopolitan. Then she arrives to this cold climate where she knows practically no one and can't speak the language. While her husband is at work she feels lonely and homesick.

Once I was invited to a Pakistani wedding which I shall never forget. It was held in a cinema. Hundreds of guests arrived in their finery, the women in bright colours displaying expensive jewellery. On the stage sat the imam, the bridegroom and other men.

The ceremony began with the priest reminding everyone of the sanctity of marriage... (But where was the bride?) The groom sat there, a lonely figure staring silently at his polished black shoes. Meanwhile the priest carried on talking, praying and giving blessings. It seemed to me that the young man was about to be married off on his own. As the tension mounted the imam suddenly announced:

- "We are now going to ask the bride's consent."

The men trooped off the stage and disappeared for twenty minutes. Meanwhile taped Urdu music kept us entertained while the restless guests chatted excitedly above the din and children ran riot.

Finally the group returned... to an expectant hush from the congregation. With a big smile on his face, the imam declared with evident relief:

- "The bride has given her consent." (Just imagine her saying 'no' at this stage!)

From the rear of the hall the bride finally emerged, walking very slowly, guided along by her women friends: she was fully covered in red, gold and orange saree material.

Now that the couple were safely married they were allowed to sit next to each other. The priest recited more prayers and blessings and then an official photographer took dozens of pictures. (This lasted another half hour.) At this stage the bride was allowed to lift the veil from her face and take a furtive look around.

The ceremony was not over yet for now the guests took it in turn to walk up to the stage and congratulate the new couple while the camera carried on flashing relentlessly.

Just as I was starting to regret not having brought my knitting along a man announced that curry and Coca-Cola were being served in a side room.

Indeed, from a Westerner's point of view, it had been a memorable wedding.

A few years ago only Africans from Nigeria, Sierra-Leone, Ghana and other ex-British colonies came to see me but now it seems that the whole of Africa is on the move. I meet people from Liberia, Ethiopia, Somalia, the Ivory Coast, Zaire, the Central African Republic - to name but a few.

An illegal immigrant told me on the phone that he had come to this country to study Accountancy but was trapped because if he did not send money home, his mother (a widow) and the rest of the family would starve. So he is condemned to be a minicab driver and can't afford to carry on with his studies.

The mistress of a prominent African politician (can't remember which country), came secretly at night in a Rolls-Royce. She was very elegant, smelt of French perfume and kept her bodyguard waiting outside, surrounding my home while she had her reading. (Admittedly, I breathed a sigh of relief when she left!)

One evening I was just going to bed when the phone stopped me in my tracks. A deep African voice sighed:

- "I am lonely and depressed so I thought I'd call you for a chat."

- "Well, it's a bit late, don't you think? Nearly midnight" I answered wearily.

- "But you MUST help me!"

It was the usual story. His family expected him to become a lawyer when, at the age of thirty, he had just failed his 'A' Levels. He hated Law anyway, but could not return to Africa as a failure.

- "Do you like cars?" I ventured.

- "I love them!" he answered enthusiastically.

- "So why don't you become a car mechanic instead? Much better to be happy in a non-academic career you enjoy rather than study a subject you find boring - it would become a life sentence."

He thought my advice over for a while then suddenly his tone of voice brightened up:

- "Yes... I am sure it's a good idea! By the way, you are a holy person. Can you pray that I find a woman? I want one NOW!"

Laughing I replied:

- "What? You want me to make one materialise for you at this time of the night? That would be a miracle indeed!"

- "You have direct communication with the Lord. Just ask him to send me one tonight. Tell him I want someone with black or brown hair and pretty - not a fat, tough, unmarried woman with six children."

- "You will just have to keep your legs crossed for the moment. Then tomorrow join a club, put an advertisement in the paper and generally go out and meet more people."

- "But if you are a medium you can make things happen much faster. Go on... say some prayers for me!"

208

- "You want a woman made to measure! Any more specifications?"

- "Yes, she must not have been used: I want her firm, fresh and plump."

Couldn't resist asking:

- "Free range?"

At least that made him laugh. He rang off in a much more cheerful frame of mind.

According to my African sitters a woman has no status until she is married and has produced at least one son. Only then is she accepted in society. They often sigh: "You can't expect a man to be faithful." They are almost resigned to this fact as father or grandfather had four wives anyway. However, this is certainly not the case with every African woman! (I am sure that many African people are happily married. But remember that I only see those who have problems).

The men show me a photograph of themselves in front of a large car. Their aim in life is to be prosperous. Those who can afford it go abroad to study or on business. Students must be prepared to spend long, lonely years away from home. The women miss the sunshine, the village life with its friendly gossip and can become very depressed.

Some African women produce a collection of three, four or even six photographs of different men:

- "This is Tom: he is in Los Angeles, studying to be an accountant. (I am in love with him)..... Now this is Dick: he is a businessman and lives back home; he is going through a divorce. He is a wealthy man with three children. (I am in love with him).... And here is Harry: he lives in London and is studying to be an engineer. (I am in love with him). Could you tell me which of the three would be the most suitable? Also which will earn the most? Would he be a good provider and make me happy?"

Several times I have heard the same story:

- "My husband says he does not find me attractive anymore. We have four children and I have always been devoted to him. Now he has a much younger woman who is expecting his child. All his spare time is spent with her. I feel so humiliated."

Naturally they are furious but only those who are financially independent can fight back. For the others this is where the witch doctor can come in handy. (Now please don't say I am making this up! All these stories are authentic.)

Africans who recently arrived in London have no concept of time - at least those I have met. They are used to living at a slower pace and probably enjoy life more. So time is not important. Two ladies from Sierra-Leone made an appointment for 11.30 a.m. At 12 one of them phoned to say they were on their way. Making sure they had written down which train to catch I then waited... and waited... until finally they arrived at 7.30 p.m. They had decided to walk instead!

Another woman made an appointment for the Saturday morning. She arrived on time... just two days late!

One or two have brought the whole family along for a great day out: not only the husband but four lively children, a sister and a friend who listen into the "private" reading.

African women are usually graceful and dignified, often highly intelligent and vivacious. (Of course I can't generalise as it is such a vast continent). Their carefully plaited hair gives them a strange beauty. Several have remained good friends over the years.

Women from Ethiopia especially have a naturally aristocratic bearing. A few of my sitters were stunning. Probably I am wrong - but they do remind me of the pictures of ladies from Ancient Egypt.

A pleasant young man from Zaire came to see me several years ago and has been phoning me regularly ever since: "My own mother is far away so I would like you to replace her."

When my eldest son answers the telephone, I see the amusement in his eyes as he calls: "Mum, it's... your third son!"

- "Bonjour, Maman, how are you today?"

I feel honoured. He has since married a West-Indian lady and they are very happy together.

A few years ago I hardly saw any Japanese in my neighbourhood but today there are more. They all seem hardworking, affluent people. The ladies who come for a reading are extremely courteous and so polite. Gracious manners and respect are very important. They bow out through the front door, inviting me to their "humble home" for a meal - which is very nice. I find it quite impossible to get the names of their ancestors!

When I meet a Chinese lady she is usually tiny, delicate, shy and very pretty. She looks only seventeen until she assures me that she is in her last year at university, taking an M.A. so I realise with a shock that she is in her late twenties. In those countries father decides which career his children are going to pursue (whether they have an aptitude for the subject or not is irrelevant). He works himself to the bone, making great sacrifices to send them abroad. The family honour is at stake so the student has no option but to succeed. At times it must seem like a life sentence.

A young sitter was very depressed because she had to retake her exams many times, failing year after year to become a chartered accountant, when, in fact her ambition was to be a fashion designer.

Another student was suicidal because he too had failed his Law exams yet again. He could not go home without qualifications: it would be too much of a disgrace. Maybe that same person would have made an excellent carpenter, but such an alternative is unthinkable.

After a few years in the West a Chinese student often starts to enjoy her freedom. Her own country suddenly feels too restricted, because tradition dictates that an unmarried girl must live with the rest of the family - usually in a small flat.

At their second appointment they offer me a box of chocolates. They are quite endearing as they join their hands and bow stiffly. It never occurs to me to bow in return! I'd rather give them a spontaneous hug which surprises and delights them.

I have met beautiful women of a mixture of races: Indian-European-Chinese-African. Once I met a fair, blue-eyed girl with blonde Afro hair and a pronounced Irish accent. There was something strangely wild about her that somehow didn't fit into the Celtic tradition. But the penny dropped when I said:

- "I am seeing the sea, the Navy. One of your ancestors sailed on a ship... it was your grandfather."

She replied:

- "Yes. Grandad came on a Merchant Navy ship from Papua, New Guinea and settled down in Ireland where he met Grandma. I don't know much about that country - only that it's somewhere near Australia."

Suddenly it all fitted into place: those strangely piercing eyes that made me feel uneasy, the aggressive personality, the frizzy hair...

Laughing, I said: "Then maybe your grandfather was a descendant of... cannibals!"

She was thrilled: "Well, that's exciting! How many other people can boast of such eccentric ancestors? You've made my day!"

In conclusion, who was the strangest person or being I have ever met? Well, my visitors come from far and wide, but this one, really I don't know exactly where he arrived from... all I know is that I won't forget him in a hurry nor do I particularly wish to see him again! To tell you the truth, the whole subject still makes me shudder.

It had started off like any other evening when, after a period of meditation I opened my eyes, feeling pleasantly relaxed... Perhaps I'd just have another cup of tea before turning in. At the kitchen door, something made me suddenly stop in my tracks, turn around and glance at the dining-room window...

There, in the soft light, floating halfway between the floor and the ceiling stood the oddest looking creature I have ever seen... silently observing me.

Startled, I froze, one hand on my mouth. Meeting a spirit was one thing but...THIS!... OH, NO!!

Goose pimples were running down my spine and arms... My visitor seemed like just another ghost... except for the face - it was not human... (At this point you may scoff: "Ha,ha! I don't believe this story." All I can say is that the presence was real and I was scared.) Should I scream and run out through the front door?... No, only idiots in films behave that way.

Throughout my life I have always taken stories of extra-terrestrials with a pinch of salt... However, this extraordinary gentleman was presumably one of them. Ghosts - the good, the bad and the ugly - none of them bother me... but I was totally unprepared for this strange guest...

He was perhaps just over 5' tall, dressed in a metallic green toga. One shoulder was bare revealing powerful muscles. This creature was bald with an outsize skull and a long pointed chin covered with a few tufts of ginger hair. But the pale face - oh dear! - was much longer and narrower than a human one, with a tiny nose and mouth and small, pointed ears. No eyes were visible, only a black hollow right across his egg-shaped face. And yet I was aware of an intelligent being's gaze scrutinising me intently...

He was cradling a white turtledove which he now gently released in the night. The spirit bird spread its wings, flew silently across the room and disappeared.

A telepathic message came to my mind:

- "You have fear of us, but we come in peace."

That was reassuring, I suppose, but at that moment in time I was far from convinced and just carried on staring at my unexpected guest. After a while he slowly disintegrated and vanished altogether. Phew! I felt quite shaken. (If you don't believe me, well that's fine. I am not trying to convince anybody. All I know is that I am telling the truth. An increasing number of people all over the world have also seen these beings.) I certainly wouldn't have wished to find myself alone in such close proximity with an extra-terrestrial. The thought still makes me feel uneasy to this day... For somehow I know this was only an introductory meeting. He will come again.

Nathan has seen these creatures too. The other evening while I was giving my son a reading, the room suddenly seemed to grow particularly cold. Looking up I noticed a triangular misty shape building up on top of his face but this time it had slanted eyes. Shuddering, I said:

- "Nathan, sit up and move, for Heaven's sake! Something is there with you."

He replied:

- "Oh, Mum, I was just going to say the same thing about you. Your face has become long and triangular, your eyes slanted slits..."

We both agreed that these beings are coming to help the world through an impending upheaval. I was reassured of their good intentions. Perhaps they are tactfully introducing themselves to the more open-minded humans, so I should be honoured. Who knows, we may end up the best of friends, but at this moment in time, I am still not sure...

Muriel on The Big Breakfast, Channel 4, with Lilly Savage and Gabriel from Brookside

Muriel on The Big Breakfast, Channel 4, with Mark Little from 'Neighbours' and Julia Carling, giving a tarot reading on Paul Gascoigne's wedding day

FREE DETAILED CATALOGUE

A detailed illustrated catalogue is available on request, SAE or International Postal Coupon appreciated. Titles are available direct from Capall Bann, post free in the UK (cheque or PO with order) or from good bookshops and specialist outlets. Titles currently available include:

Angels and Goddesses - Celtic Christianity & Paganism by Michael Howard
Arthur - The Legend Unveiled by C Johnson & E Lung
Auguries and Omens - The Magical Lore of Birds by Yvonne Aburrow
Cats' Company by Ann Walker
Celtic Lore & Druidic Ritual by Rhiannon Ryall
Celtic Saints and the Glastonbury Zodiac by Mary Caine
Crystal Clear - A Guide to Quartz Crystal by Jennifer Dent
Earth Dance - A Year of Pagan Rituals by Jan Brodie
Earth Harmony - Places of Power, Holiness and Healing by Nigel Pennick
Earth Magic by Margaret McArthur
Enchanted Forest - The Magical Lore of Trees by Yvonne Aburrow
Familiars - Animal Powers of Britain by Anna Franklin
Handbook of Fairies by Ronan Coghlan
Healing Homes by Jennifer Dent
Herbcraft - Shamanic & Ritual Use of Herbs by Susan Lavender & Anna Franklin
In Search of Herne the Hunter by Eric Fitch
Inner Space Workbook - Developing Counselling & Magical Skills Through the Tarot
Living Tarot by Ann Walker
Magical Lore of Cats by Marion Davies
Magical Lore of Herbs by Marion Davies
Mysteries of the Runes by Michael Howard
Mystic Life of Animals by Ann Walker
Patchwork of Magic by Julia Day
Pathworking - A Practical Book of Guided Meditations by Pete Jennings
Pickingill Papers - The Origins of Gardnerian Wicca by Michael Howard
Practical Spirituality by Steve Hounsome
Psychic Animals by Dennis Bardens
Psychic Self Defence - Real Solutions by Jan Brodie
Runic Astrology by Nigel Pennick
Sacred Animals by Gordon MacLellan
Sacred Grove - The Mysteries of the Forest by Yvonne Aburrow
Sacred Geometry by Nigel Pennick
Sacred Lore of Horses The by Marion Davies
Seasonal Magic - Diary of a Village Witch by Paddy Slade
Secret Places of the Goddess by Philip Heselton
Talking to the Earth by Gordon Maclellan
Taming the Wolf - Full Moon Meditations by Steve Hounsome
The Goddess Year by Nigel Pennick & Helen Field
West Country Wicca by Rhiannon Ryall

Capall Bann is owned and run by people actively involved in many of the areas in which we publish. Our list is expanding rapidly so do contact us for details on the latest releases.

Capall Bann Publishing, Freshfields, Chieveley, Berks, RG20 8TF